If you have ever listened to a symphony orchestra in a concert hall or on the radio, if you have ever played in a band, tried to write a song, bought a classical record, or even sung a bit of opera in the shower, this book will provide information and entertainment for you. It tells something about conductors, composers, publishers, concert artists, managers, ASCAP, copyright, records, opera, and compositions of all sorts; it contains facts, figures, anecdotes, and personal reminiscences, and touches on almost every phase of music in modern America.

This is the story of one day in the busy life of a prominent music publisher, H. W. Heinsheimer, a man who knows all the outstanding personalities in his field and is thoroughly familiar with every variation on the theme of music in this country.

"Music," says Mr. Heinsheimer, "is falling on the soil of America like a steady, gentle rain." He shows how, within a scant thirty years, music has penetrated the heart of this country; how great European performers and composers have come here to make their homes; how our own local talent has flourished; and how local symphonies, choral societies, and opera groups have sprung up in communities all over the nation. He also details the story of the growth of the giant concert bureaus which have become the "mightiest music-producing machines in the world, welding three million Americans into one big, happy organized audience."

FANFARE
FOR
2 PIGEONS

By H. W. HEINSHEIMER

FANFARE FOR 2 PIGEONS

MENAGERIE IN F SHARP

FANFARE

FOR

2 PIGEONS

BY

H. W. HEINSHEIMER

DOUBLEDAY & COMPANY, INC., GARDEN CITY, NEW YORK, 1952

16115 '83

Some of the material used in this book has previously been used in magazine articles. Sections of Chapter II have appeared in *Holiday*, sections of Chapter VIII in *Tomorrow*, and sections of Chapters XII and XIII in the *Musical Quarterly*.

CONTENTS

FANFARE

FOR

2 PIGEONS

Beethoven

ON

FORTY-THIRD STREET

Brakes scream, horns bark impatiently, the traffic cop's motorcycle sputters through the street. From the east the whistle of the doorman at the Biltmore Hotel, imploring, desperate, persistent. From the west the whistle of the policeman on Fifth Avenue, the cling-clang of home-coming fire trucks, the roar of buses. Stop,go, stop,go, stop,go— and every time the surging crescendo of a million spark plugs.

Drivers of gargantuan trucks purple-faced and in vain shouting for a little *Lebensraum*. Seventy empty metal containers, seventy exploding cymbals, hurled on the sidewalk in front of the Brass Rail restaurant by a merrily singing Negro boy. The *Times*, the *News*, the *Mirror*, the *Journal-American*: get it here, read it all, get it, get it, get it.

Bits of Waldteufel and Delibes come floating from the dome of the National City

Bank, mingling with the trembling reflections of hymn tunes from the Fifth Church of Christ, Scientist. And the unending shuffle of feet, grinding over the gum-splattered asphalt, thousands, hundred thousands, released from the never-resting gates of Grand Central—soft memories of Mount Kisco morning dew still in the hearts of their owners, of an early begonia, a rabbit across the road, a woodpecker in a sun-kissed garden, but the feet already tired, grinding wearily to work.

Shouts, whistles, horns, songs, cries, laughter, brakes, cycles, power drills, the incessant small-arm fire of talk, millions of cars, millions of feet, shuffling, grinding, thumping, hurrying, hurrying, hurrying by.

And above it all: Beethoven! Every morning as I emerge from the inferno of the shuttle train into the trembling light of the street I am greeted by the gold-coated head, resting broadly and secure on a window ledge on Forty-third Street in Manhattan, between Madison and Fifth. It gives me a good feeling and prepares me soothingly for the day to see him there, proud and great and very silent, never touched by the swirling river of noise that roars incessantly through the street.

And it makes me smile, happily, when I follow his frowning stare. Beethoven looks straight—and, when the light is right, it seems not at all without interest—into the tellers' room of the Emigrant Industrial Savings Bank!

I wave at him as a friend waves at a friend. He doesn't respond. He just looks ahead, at the adding machines, the pretty hostesses, gently swaying to the sounds of Muzak, and at millions and millions of money.

The cop on Fifth Avenue whistles lustily. The traffic grinds to a stop. I spot a crack between the bumpers and dive across the street.

The house of G. Schirmer, music publishers, dealers, and importers, is a seven-story building, devoted exclusively to the cause of music. Beethoven up there on the second floor works for them. So do I.

When I enter through the revolving doors, walking through the store on my way to my office, I am already in a happy, expectant mood. The place is clean and shiny, pleasant in its colors and proportions. The street, as soon as I enter, seems miles away. It is quiet here, peaceful, cool. As I walk up the little winding stair towards my room on the mezzanine, a shower of music comes sprinkling down from the second floor (Records and Albums, Needles, Cabinets, Carrying Cases and Accessories) where a phonograph plays sections from *The Messiah* or the Coronation Scene from *Boris Godounow* or something else beautiful and majestic and good to begin the day with.

Down in the store piano teachers perch on comfortable stools, wise old owls, gaily feathered cockatoos, and many a cute little chick, thumbing through neat folders bulging with music. Slow-moving, white-haired gentlemen slide on soundless soles behind the counters, winding their unerring way through rows and rows of gleaming steel files. They know every piece of music ever written, every composer from Albéniz to Zimbalist, every key and arrangement, title and publisher, price and edition, out of print, back in print, back in stock, out of stock, yes madam, no madam—gentle, fatherly, never in doubt, never a loud word, never a gesture of irritation, every customer a lifelong friend, chick and owl alike. And when, after hours of hushed conversation, they have to ring the cash register on a 37-cent sale, they do it with hesitation, visibly afraid the harsh commercial sound may indecently disturb the atmosphere.

Next, at the Vocal Counter, the booming voices of huge bassos clash with the giggle of half a dozen of the Lily Ponses of the sixties. Opera stars and passers-through from Hollywood patiently wait their turn, rubbing mink coats with Juilliard undergraduates, church singers from Harlem, a night-club chanteuse, a couple of starved-looking accompanists. A long-legged, pale-faced ballerina from Sioux City affects a heavy Russian accent. A retired primadonna under a tremendous green straw hat talks powerfully beneath a make-up that has seen many a better day.

A little further on, two salesmen who in decades of dealing with organists, choirmasters, and representatives of the White Plains Board of Education have taken on the solemn appearance of friendly vestrymen talk in whispers to a tiny, heavily veiled nun. I don't know their names but I am almost certain that one of them answers to the name of Requiem while the other one appears on the payroll as Gloria in Excelsis or simply Magnificat.

Right next to them—they never look that way—is "popular," screaming in hellish purple, indecent pink, rude apple green, pushy, nymphomanic blue.

The book department, brilliant in its colors, bristles with books on music and musicians, with pictures and little marble busts and magazines of all sizes, shapes, and languages. Every morning I take a quick look to see how many copies of my own books are still in stock. I know the exact spot where they keep them and can take a quick count from the corner of my eye while walking by nonchalantly. Seven copies I count on Monday, seven on Tuesday, seven still on Wednesday. But on Thursday, oh happy day, I count only six, and Mr. West comes over to tell me that he sold one to a lady from Idaho.

There are gleaming guitars in the store, elegant little organs, metronomes and shiny trumpets, and musical toys: horses and mules, big white poodles and red riding-hoods, and hundreds of music boxes that fill the place with a sweet soft tingle of Mary Had a Little Lamb and The Blue Bells of Scotland. Right in the center, facing the street, is the information booth, occupied by two absolutely overwhelming-looking blondes. Miss Carmignano and Miss Love are the two people I see first every morning—first, that is, after I have seen Beethoven. What could be nicer than to work in a place where you first see Beethoven, and then a beautiful girl named Love?

When I close the door of my office behind me, the Blue Bells of Scotland cease to ring. On the desk I see the merry pile of morning mail. As I walk towards it I can already spot the promising silk of foreign air-mail paper, the intriguing shape of telegrams, sheets and sheets of letters, neatly opened and appetizingly stacked up, concert programs, posters, magazines—each of them, I know, full of adventure and excitement—each of them telling a story that goes beyond the dry, businesslike message they may contain.

The dean of Indiana University reports on the success of a new American opera whose world première he just gave with his students. Oak Ridge, a brand-new city, has a brand-new symphony, and here is a letter from its conductor, Waldo Cohn, atomic chemist, cello player, music fanatic. Here are press reports on performances of an American opera from Stockholm, London, Berlin.

A two-hundred-word telegram from Hollywood, which could have been, just as well, a gentle postcard, screams hysterically from the top of the pile.

Bands in colorful uniforms march out of the papers on my desk, whirling, beautiful majorettes, cornet players with serious eyes—the windows rattle as millions join the parade. There comes a somber procession of widows, nephews, a lawyer from Shreveport, a couple of bespectacled judges—participants all in a fascinating lawsuit for infringement of copyright—more fascinating than the juiciest case of adultery, murder, rape. Records of new American symphonies look out of scurrile covers. The whirling contours of dancers are silhouetted against the wall. From the silent pictures on the wall come the voices

of forever silent friends—Alban Berg, Béla Bartók, Kurt
Weill. . . .

It is time to begin the day. Through the window I can
see an architect's empty workshop, a row of naked dummies in a dressmaker's dreary atelier, a girl, tired, pale,
shriveled, making a hectic telephone call. On the window
sill my two pigeons, Major and Minor, their rainbow-
speckled feathers fighting a gallant battle with the grime
that comes seeping down the courtyard like black snow.
They always sit there, looking at the papers and manuscripts on my desk. They know more about modern music
than any two pigeons in the whole world and, for quite
some time, their cooing has sounded like two-part inven-
tions, slightly jazzed up with a lot of wrong basses.

I close the window and sit down at my desk. For a
short moment, before the day engulfs me, I try to think
about the meaning of all these letters—of the people behind them, the ideas, the thoughts, the battles, the
dreams that make their hearts beat, the music that makes
them dream their dreams. As I look again, the girl on the
telephone, the staring dummies, the architect's dusty
tables are gone. The voice of the turtle has been stilled. I
can see, instead, a wide magnificent landscape and hear
music falling on it, steady, like a gentle rain.

LANDSCAPE
IN
THE RAIN

Like a steady gentle rain, music is falling on the soil of America.

Only a little while ago the land out there was parched, a barren land untouched by the beauty and the dream, the happiness and oblivion, the rapture and the uplifting excitement that only music brings to man. Now it blossoms and sprouts, green and fertile, irrigated by friendly streams, merry cascades, majestic rivers of music.

In the hills of the Berkshires, fifteen thousand visitors assemble on the nocturnal lawn, roofed by the quiet breath of the Great Dipper, gently touched by the hum of distant airplanes, to drink in solemn concentration the refreshing strains of great music. The palms and flowers, trees and stone walls of the Hollywood Bowl, the Robin Hood Dell, of big parks in Chicago, Boston, New Orleans, New York reflect the voices of singers, the beat of dancing feet, the echoes of trumpets and kettledrums.

Throughout the land, trains and planes carry traveling artists: pianists, dancers, composers, old ladies playing the harpsichord, singers, string quartets, opera companies. The twenty professional symphony orchestras that played to the citizens of a few big cities in 1920 have grown to one hundred and fifty, spread all across the continent. Centers of musical learning, attracting students from all over the world, have sprung up—hundreds of them.

The great masters of the baton, the great performers and composers no longer come to these shores only to pick up a hatful of hastily collected dollars and then to return to their homelands. Arturo Toscanini's address is Riverdale, New York. Bruno Walter's home isn't in Vienna any more: it is in Beverly Hills. Serge Koussevitzky had become a stranger in Paris but he wasn't a stranger in Lenox. A Massachusetts mountainside became his chosen resting place.

Igor Stravinsky lives and writes in Los Angeles, Paul Hindemith in New Haven, Darius Milhaud in Oakland, Bohuslav Martinu in Princeton, Alexander Tscherepnine in Chicago. Gian-Carlo Menotti, Italian, got his musical education in Philadelphia and writes his operas in English. In a complete reversal of traditional traffic rules, they are first produced in America and exported from here, on unprecedented trips, to the stages of Germany, Italy, or Scandinavia.

The Budapest Quartet hasn't been in Budapest for a very long time.

But there is more music out there—not quite as refined, maybe, as polished and civilized, but full of real life and real joy and refreshing, heart-warming beauty. It is music that cannot be bought for all the money and all the wealth in the world. It doesn't make headlines in the trade papers and isn't quoted among the merchants at the musical stock market, on Fifty-seventh Street in New York. I can hear the gentle knock of the baton as a rehearsal gets under way in Lincoln High Auditorium somewhere in any one of a hundred anonymous towns.

The hum of the voices dies down. The oboe player— Mr. Roy Marshall, funeral director—rises to sound a proudly sustained A. Students unwrap their clarinets, young ladies settle tenderly with fiddles and trombones. Doctors and plumbers, nurses and mail carriers, the butcher and the baker open the first page of the *Unfinished Symphony*. Where is Mrs. Helms? There she is, pushing her way through the empty seats of the auditorium, covered with instrument cases, coats, rubber boots, getting out her cello, rushing up to the podium. Don't blush, Mrs. Helms, don't worry, we'll wait. We have no Toscanini here but no Petrillo either. We have time. We know you had to make dinner first and put the children to bed. We are happy to have you here. Sit down, Mrs. Helms, relax. You and your cello, you are leading off tonight—right here, at the beginning of the symphony. Forget the dishes, the children, the house, the world. Play, Mrs. Helms, *espressivo, dolce,* with all your heart and all your love, your tears and your smiles, *piano, espressivo, dolce* . . .

Now a mightier sound floats by—the voices of four hundred friends of music, getting together in San Francisco, or Portland, or Salt Lake, or Chapel Hill to sing Verdi's *Requiem,* the *Missa Solemnis,* the *Children's Crusade.* And the bands, twenty-five thousand bands in high schools and colleges. And the new opera workshops, hundreds of them, training singers, pounding out the music of immortal operas on creaky pianos, hammering away at primitive scenery, sewing costumes, pasting beards, dancing, fencing, singing, having a wonderful, wonderful time.

That is the music that fertilizes the land, liberates the souls, makes the tired faces radiant with happiness. It's free as the air, healthy and nourishing as an apple picked up by the wayside, stimulating and quickening the hearts like a long, wonderful kiss in the dark on the front porch, before a trembling hand, gloved again, rings the paternal doorbell and an announcement on Cartier stationery makes it all legal, expensive, and dull.

Thirty years ago, all this didn't exist. Scarcely were its contours discernible. Today it is here, no longer a dream but clear, resounding reality. Within the span of one human generation, music has become a deeply integrated part of American life.

It is new, sudden, and in all its makings terribly unorthodox. It started out and has grown up, almost completely ignoring what used to be an axiom of musical growth all over the world, valid for centuries and never seriously challenged: that the administration and the support of music was a public duty. In Europe, what had been started by emperors, kings, and the princes of the church has been taken up by cities, counties, and states. Every major community allots a subsidy to their opera house, their orchestra, their music schools. Neither war nor revolution, occupation nor famine was allowed to interfere with what is considered an inescapable obligation. The Vienna Philharmonic and the Vienna State Opera are part of the city as are the trees and churches and the old palaces. Emperors would go, republics fall into the dust, dictators would goose-step down the boulevards and foreign soldiers chase out the dictators, and still the government—the emperor, the republic, the dictator, the pathetic little men surrounded by the bayonets of the conqueror—paid for music as if time had stood still.

The Federal Music Project of the Works Progress Administration of the New Deal was the closest America has come so far towards a publicly subsidized and publicly administered musical life. At its height, in 1936, the United States Government supported thirty-six federal symphony orchestras in addition to teaching units, choral and opera groups, chamber-music ensembles, dance orchestras, composer forums, and bands. More than fifteen thousand musicians, working in nearly seven hundred different projects, were on the federal payroll.

After a few years which saw the blossoming of many wild, beautiful flowers (tied up, however, by plenty of red tape into regulation-size bouquets), it all vanished. Reminiscences remained: many of the WPA orchestras were maintained as community orchestras, and here and there—lately, under the impact of changing economic conditions, increasingly so—attempts are being made to translate public interest in music into public responsibility. Slowly these trends begin to take on serious significance.

The city of Philadelphia, for instance, now gives a yearly grant of fifty thousand dollars to its orchestra. In return, the orchestra plays four free concerts at Convention Hall, owned by the city and seating sixteen thousand people. The Philadelphia newspapers print coupons, and anybody wishing to attend clips one out and sends in his application. There is a limit of two concerts to each coupon and of four tickets for each coupon clipper. Schools and hospitals can secure a whole block of seats. There are no reserved seats in Convention Hall. For every concert the demand exceeds the hall's huge capacity.

In Sioux City a special orchestra tax is levied. It yields between ten and twelve thousand dollars for the local symphony. Los Angeles County gives a small amount, more a token than a real subsidy, but important as a token, towards the maintenance of a local opera company. The cities of Denver, Indianapolis, Baltimore, San

Francisco, St. Louis, Buffalo, Rochester (New York), Houston, and a few others give cash subsidies to their orchestras or help in the form of free use of auditoriums, of instruments, office space, music libraries, and promotion. In New Orleans the city as well as the Board of Education supports the orchestra. In the budget of the state of North Carolina—between an appropriation for Fugitives from Justice, who for some strange reason get three thousand dollars per annum, and the Confederate Cemetery, which gets three hundred and fifty—appears a subsidy of fifteen thousand dollars for the North Carolina Symphony and thirty thousand dollars for the Brevard Music Foundation, Inc., sponsors of one of the most enterprising and spirited music camps and festivals in the land.

The most important indication of a significant change in the fortunes of the arts in America, however, is the action of the 82d Congress to do away with the 20 per cent admission tax for events given by "a society or organization conducted for the sole purpose of maintaining symphony orchestras or operas and receiving substantial support from voluntary contributions." The immediate monetary importance of the new law is obvious. It has all but saved many institutions. The effect on the Metropolitan Opera can be considered typical for all of them: in its last season before the tax was abolished it had a deficit of $462,000. It paid slightly more than that in admission taxes to the federal government! The Philadelphia Orchestra, in the same period of time, had a deficit of $45,520 and paid $60,495 in admission taxes.

The significance of the new law seems, however, to go far beyond these immediate considerations. That the tax repeal should have occurred at a time when taxes were raised, not lowered, and certainly not done away with altogether, more determinedly than ever before in the history of the land, seems an important token of a new attitude of the Congress and the Government towards the arts and particularly towards music. Already there is talk about a Secretary of the Fine Arts, and several bills have been introduced, all aiming towards an even more direct and constructive support of the arts than was already so clearly displayed in the new tax law. At the hearing that preceded the enactment of the law, Mr. Floyd G. Blair, president and treasurer of the Philharmonic Symphony Society of New York, made a passionate statement before the House Finance Committee. Referring to the activities of hundreds of orchestras, thousands of community and civic groups, and to the millions who listen to musical broadcasts and enjoy the records of our great orchestras, he asked the lawmakers:

"What does this mean to the American people? Is it really important to continue? Is it something that in times of stress and worry people had better do without? Is it something we should deny our youth? Is it something which should be grouped with movies and perhaps night clubs? Or is it part of our cultural education, something that touches the soul, something which with many approaches the realm of religion?

"If you have any doubts as to the answer to these questions, I can resolve them. Each Sunday one hundred radio stations carry our broadcasts to the people of the nation. Each Sunday we appeal to the radio audiences for financial help. We receive thousands of letters from people in all walks of life. As so often is the case, those who can least afford it make the greatest sacrifice to help us."

Mr. Blair—not a long-haired crackpot but a vice-president of the National City Bank—then read a few of these letters which, he said, "show better than any words of mine can convey what music means to the people of this country." The letters from North Hollywood, from Erie, from a worker in Saint Meinrad Abbey, Indiana, from Detroit and Bay City and Telford, Pennsylvania, and Rome, New York, are now part of the records of the United States Congress. The words that were spoken will not be erased. The tax has been repealed today. Tomorrow . . .

But tomorrow isn't here, yet. All these are still only straws in the wind, the first whiffs of a still distant spring, deviations from the basic principle, still valid and still generally accepted, that music in America is the concern of the individual, not of a public agency.

Each year drives get under way in hundreds of towns to help the local symphony. Men's clubs are organized, young people's subsidiaries, and, above all, women's auxiliaries. Six hundred ladies get together—in St. Louis, for example. They elect a president, two vice-presidents,

a corresponding and a recording secretary. That leaves
595 members unelected. They go to work, organizing
themselves into committees, so numerous, so colorful
that prose alone will not suffice to do them justice. Greet-
ings, then, to the St. Louis Women's Association and to
all other Women's Associations of all the Symphony
Orchestras of America and their *Seventeen Committees.*

Solo *very rhythmical:*
    Finance
    Biennial Conference
    Arrangements
    Education.

        Chorus *shouting:*
           And the Biennial Conference Committee
               prepares
           The Biennial Conference of all
           The Women's Associations of all
           The Symphony Orchestras of all
           The United States.

Solo *gentle, lyrical, con amore:*
    Revisions
    Hospitality
    Publicity
    And phone.

        Chorus *slow with expression:*
           And the Telephone Committee mans six
               telephones
           In a West End Office

> In a West End Office
> And makes six thousand telephone calls
> To six thousand prospects
> To six thousand prospects
> Every year.

Solo *fast:*
  Membership
  Radio
  Program
  Students Concerts.

> Chorus *tempo di Morse:*
> And the Radio Committee conducts
> A weekly radio quiz program
> To which the listeners send in questions
> To be answered by
>   (*unisono, fortissimo*) an outstanding
>   authority.

Solo *very fast:*
  The vicinity committee!
  The scholarship committee!
  The guest speakers committee!
  The entertainment committee and . . .

> Chorus *interrupting, exuberantly:*
> The scholarship committee
> Sells tickets
> So that a worthy student can get a schol-
>   arship.
> While the vicinity committee
> Sells tickets
> In the vicinity.

Solo and chorus *maestoso*:

  . . . and the presidentsofthepastsixyearsadvisorycommittee,
    The Presidents Of The Past Six Years Advisory
      Committee!
    Which is a committee
    Formed by the presidents
    Of the past six years
    To give
    Advice.

What happens in St. Louis happens all over America.
For every musical casualty two new organizations spring
up. There never seems an end to it. No city government
or state supervisor tells the orchestra of Springfield,
Massachusetts, how to conduct its affairs, but when funds
are running low, Mrs. Douglas V. Wallace, an officer of
the association, invites everybody in town to come and
have a look at her new home on Longmeadow Street, a
"modernistic" house that had been the talk of the town.
Three thousand people pass through the building, each
one shaking hands with the hostess and leaving a dollar
at the door, to save the Springfield Symphony.

During a few hectic war months the government built
the town of Oak Ridge. Seventy-five thousand people
were settled, overnight, within its brand-new confines.
The government provided houses and streets, libraries
and drugstores. It didn't provide for music. When the
town was six months old, Oak Ridge had a sixty-man
orchestra, a civic chorus, and a chamber music group;
every one of the players and singers worked in one of the

atomic factories or was an Oak Ridge housewife. The conductor was a chemist who spent his days close to the atomic stock pile and his evenings with a baton and a stack of music and a group of eager men and women who had come to make music before the paint of their houses was dry and the red Tennessee clay had been transformed into passable streets.

In Oklahoma City they have stopped selling tickets for the concerts of their Symphony Orchestra. The desire to buy a ticket to hear a celebrated visiting artist is not sufficient to qualify for admission. You have to do more to discharge your duties towards music and the cultural demands of the community: you have to become part of the musical community by signing up as a member of the Oklahoma State Symphony Orchestra, Inc. Only then are you admitted to the concerts. There are regular memberships for twenty-five dollars, fellowships at half price, and student memberships for as little as five dollars. Out-of-towners—some of them travel hundreds of miles to participate in the musical events—are given special membership rates. The members of the society—and the members only—have free admission to all the concerts of the orchestra. They can also come and hear—again for free—the concerts of the Little Symphony, a smaller body of players who perform for them serenades by Mozart, symphonies by Haydn, pieces by contemporary composers. Hundreds of young people from the state university and from colleges in and around the town join with the orchestra in performances of oratorios. Five thousand citizens of Oklahoma have joined the drive for more and better music in a city that only a few years ago was concerned mostly with more and better cows, oil, and corn.

Strange things are happening. The town of Louisville, Kentucky, twice recently made news in national magazines. It wasn't made by the galloping ponies at Churchill Downs, but by the local orchestra's daring and brilliantly executed plan to replace the roster of famous soloists appearing with live composers. New works were commissioned for a fraction of the price the usual stellar attraction would have demanded, and most of them presented in the presence of the composer. No high-priced, traveling virtuoso has done for the musical pride, for the feeling of accomplishment and cultural independence, what the visits of outstanding composers, their stay in the town, their contact with its musical and spiritual leaders, have done.

In Albuquerque, New Mexico—but there must be a letter, somewhere, on my desk, among the papers. Let's get it out.

Here it is. It comes from a young man by the name of Kurt Frederick, a native of Austria. "A few years ago," he writes, "while I was conductor of the Albuquerque Civic Symphony, I read in a newspaper that Arnold Schönberg had finished a new composition, *A Survivor from Warsaw*, for chorus, narration, and orchestra. I wrote to him and asked for the score.

"He sent it, telling me in a letter that the work had not yet been performed and that I could play it with my

group as a world première if I wished to. Imagine! Schönberg *premières* used to take place in Vienna, in Berlin,
in Prague—this was Albuquerque, New Mexico. The orchestra was an amateur organization. University and
high-school students played in it and a few people from
the town.

"We started rehearsals. I can't tell you how many we
had—after the first three dozen I stopped counting. The
lines the chorus had to sing are set to Hebrew words. Our
chorus consisted of people from the city, some university
students, and a group from Estancia, a community of
668 souls in an isolated district, mostly farmers. They
were trained for our performance by the local high-school
teacher. To attend rehearsals they had to drive fifty-five
miles each way.

"I have played modern music in New York and other
big cities. Never have I encountered such a humble attitude of appreciation and respect as among the amateurs
of our small community. While the chorus was struggling
with the text and the tremendous difficulties of intoning
this strange music I never heard a joke, never a disparag-
ing remark. After four months of preparations we felt
ourselves ready to perform the work. At the end I scarcely
believed my ears as I heard the applause. This was difficult music, atonal, uncompromising, harsh on ears and
nerves. But the people seemed genuinely moved by its
impact, deeply attentive, eager to participate in a new
experience.

"The narrator—a professor of chemistry at the University of New Mexico—asked the listeners whether they wished to hear the work a second time. The applause increased in intensity. We repeated the piece. Not one of the fifteen hundred people that crowded our hall left before the end."

This is a big and powerful movement, a great, sweeping event. It is the cultural liberation of the American hinterland, its emancipation from the big cities, its growth into uncountable independent musical units no longer shaped by what is going on in New York's Carnegie Hall, refusing to accept as their supreme judgment the music column of a metropolitan newspaper or the verdict of a metropolitan salesman, striving to form their own cultural destiny after the heart and mind, the tastes and demands of their own people.

American universities have become the closest counterpart to the princely Maecenas of the European past. New auditoriums are growing, teachers are being assembled from all over the world. Experiments in every branch of musical activity are undertaken with imagination, free from the strangulating pressure of box-office considerations. Composers are encouraged with prizes and stipends; many of them have been given security as composers in residence to give them time to create at leisure, relieved from the worries of the day, and to pass on their knowledge and experience, the impact of a creative personality, so impossible to evaluate in working hours or "practical" results. Already in Bloomington, in Urbana, in Ann Arbor, Stanford, Denver, Seattle, New Orleans, and in scores of other universities a thriving musical life is growing in intensity, quality, and ambition.

A great number of these schools have elaborate opera departments, orchestras, chamber-music groups, laboratories of musical learning. Fine orchestra players are being engaged as faculty members and then loaned to the local symphony orchestra, which could never afford to hire members of such quality and whose standard is immeasurably raised by their participation. Other universities have string quartets in residence—some of them ensembles of international fame—who teach a few hours each week and give concerts on the campus but otherwise have a lavishly allocated amount of time for themselves— to study, to rehearse, and, most important, to just live and grow as musicians. When they travel across the land they carry the message of fine music and good will for the alma mater with them. Nothing else is expected from them. One of these string quartets, formed by graduates of New York's Juilliard School of Music and maintained by the institution whose name it carries, is made up of four ridiculously young players who look and act and play as never a European string quartet looked and acted and played—violent, obsessed, magnificently independent, inspiringly unrestrained—symbols and messengers of a new spirit.

Look at these four boys when you look for music in America—don't look only at the refined accomplishments of world-famous orchestras, at the recordings of brilliant voices and expensive Stradivarius violins, at the great maestro's impeccable music coming over the air. Don't look for the smooth, the refined, the finished, the impeccable, the polished, the aged. Come and listen to the St. Matthew Passion, performed by three hundred and fifty students of the University of Salt Lake City. Listen to a Youth Concert in Los Angeles. Sneak in at a rehearsal of the concert band of the University of Michigan. Come to Logan, Utah, a town of twelve thousand, when the visiting orchestra from Salt Lake stops for two concerts—one for four thousand children in the afternoon and one for four thousand grownups in the evening. Mingle with the players when Igor Stravinsky conducts the University Orchestra in Urbana, Illinois. Take your seat at the Lewisohn Stadium in New York and look at the faces of the tired men in shirt sleeves and the tired women in blouse and skirt, sprawled on the empty stones in the suffocating heat of an August night; look at their faces and see what happens to them when Heifetz, small, pathetic figure down in the shell, begins to play the Brahms concerto.

You can hear the music all over America. It is here and it won't go again.

It has taken hold of the hearts of the people. Like a gentle rain it is coming from the clouds. The people step out of their houses and workshops, from the noisy buses, the clatter of machines, the monotony of typewriters, the long, long wait for the streetcar.

They lift their tired faces and smile.

Melody

IN F

IN C

Major and Minor have returned to their window. Their mother-of-pearl eyes eagerly memorize the jagged lines of a love song on my desk that came in with the morning mail and will go back to the composer—I know it but sentimental Minor doesn't—before the sun will set. The architect's drawing tables, empty still, are back where they belong. And there is the tired, shriveled girl again, still clutching the phone, her soundless lips moving hysterically, her sickly hand hammering home unknown messages of despair.

The sound of the rain has stopped.

Instead, there is thunder over my head, heavy, rumbling, prolonged. It is the mailman, unloading, as he does every day, his heavy bag of musical manuscripts on the worn-out carpet of the Publication Department. I count at least twenty packages landing heavily on the floor above. It is the usual average for the day: five thousand citizens, year after year, mail the products of their musical fancy to a house such as this in the unshakable expectation of getting them published. Each of the five thousand packages contains from one to twenty different compositions, an average of 12,579 manuscripts submitted for publication in an average year. Leap years, of course, do better.

Composing, or, to use a more adequate formulation, drawing dots and lines on five staves and calling the result opus 34, has become a great contemporary pastime. There just doesn't seem to be anybody left in this great land who can read the Twenty-third Psalm, see a rosebud in June, woo a fair maid, or pass an ol' cotton, saw, wind, steel, wood, paper, or gin mill without breaking out in melody and mailing the result by registered post to a music publisher.

Manuscripts roll in from cities and hamlets, from mountain cabins and ocean shores, from ships at sea and planes aloft. They come from the rich and the poor, the sophisticated and the simple, from men, women, and babes. Coal miners write music and so do headwaiters at the Roosevelt Hotel, and as for housewives—housewives certainly compose galore.

There are manuscripts scrawled on scraps of stained note paper in the timid stumble of the teen-ager or the trembling drawl of the octogenarian, elaborate oratorios of three hundred pages, drawn in heartbreaking calligraphy, simple ditties written without the help of chords or bar lines, in pencils of all colors, in ink and paint of every shade—heaps, mountains, himalayas of music, and never an end in sight.

Only about a hundred (and that is a good and fertile year, a fine and promising harvest) are accepted and published, or, to be more accurate, are accepted and sometimes even published. The recipients of the 12,479 rejection slips resent them bitterly, of course. They don't mind that it takes ten years of hard labor to become a successful waiter—not even a headwaiter—at the Roosevelt Hotel, but are firmly convinced that all they need to be a successful composer is a song in their hearts and the back of a menu to scribble it on. When the menu comes back with a letter as chilly as vichyssoise, they find consolation in the thought that their manuscripts were never looked on at all, or were rejected by stupid, corrupt and/or jealous men who probably copied them secretly before sending them back, or who deliberately closed their ears to the artistic beauty and commercial potentialities of the hit song of the century.

No one should indulge in such pleasant illusions. The times—if ever there were such times, and history has little to prove it—when talent would wither, an undiscovered violet, till a distant heir discovered and brought to fame fabulous musical treasures hidden in faded notebooks, these times are gone, and for good. Today, consumption and dissemination of music in every form has taken on such fantastic proportions that no talent, be it ever so frail, will go undiscovered. There is a niche for anyone.

The twelve-tone recluse has his chance as well as the hill-billy.

A composer's output might elude the combined eagle eyes of all the music publishers who are the consecutive recipients of every rejected manuscript: there is still a veritable army of possible discoverers, sponsors, exploit-ers, or just loiterers on the musical market. Radio and film need music in unheard-of quantities; so do Muzak and disk jockeys, contests and prizes, ballet companies and band competitions, Leagues of Composers and In-ternational Societies for Contemporary Music, recording companies springing up like mushrooms in every corner of the land, composers' forums and laboratories, whatever those are. There are artists anxious to attract the critics by including a World First, American First, or at least East Lansing First on their recital programs, workshops thriv-ing on the meticulous preparation and spirited presenta-tion of new operas, chamber music ensembles, and con-ductors, eager to show their allegiance to the town which pays their salaries by performing the new score of a native, be it ever so humble (and it usually is).

All these forces and many more are forever dragging a narrow-meshed net through the musical ocean. Any fish of respectable size will get caught. He might be thrown back and never have another chance; but once he will see the brilliant sun, once, for a short moment, be singled out before vanishing again, forever, in the anonymous depth. Those who never get caught better go home and give up trying to be a tuna. They are sunfish, at best, and should live accordingly.

Music publishers, certainly, try hard and persistently to catch what they think worth catching. There are men on their staff, editors, who, all their lives, look at nothing but choral music, called "octavo" in the trade. Octavo! The word will haunt them forever, filling their aging hearts with the violent desire to make ship for Trinidad and the islands of the south, to fill their lungs with the smell of salt water, to live with a girl high up on the cliff where they can see the sun dip in the water and the little white boats dance in the bay—any girl as long as she will never mention octavo. But they never find her. They keep looking at octavo instead, Monday to Friday from 9.30 to 5. Secular Unison, Sacred Unison, Secular Mixed, Sacred Mixed, Secular a cappella, Sacred a cappella, Secular SA, Sacred SA, Secular and Sacred SS, SSA, TB, TTBB, SAB, SATB, SSAATTBB—not, as one would hope, an array of interesting diseases or of pretty, promising curse words, but abbreviations for every conceivable combination of Sopranos, Altos, Tenors, and Basses. The devastating monotony of their days is occasionally interrupted by a few carelessly thrown in cantatas, masses, kol nidres, pageants, te deums, oratorios, and a ton or two of dirges.

There are other editors whose job it is to peruse songs. Incoming songs are about equally divided between what the composers blasphemously believe to be a song pleasing to the Lord (sacred) and those in which they express more earth-bound feelings, mostly love of woman, man, mountains, country, flora and fauna, with birds and canines heavily outnumbering insects and aquatics. Others attempt a strictly humorous approach towards life. Songs dealing with love and humor are called secular songs and are dedicated *To Mabel, To John Without Whom This Song Would Never Have Been Written*, or to *R.T., lovingly*. Sacred songs are dedicated *To Mother* (81 per cent) or to *The St. Olaf Lutheran Gesangsverein* (19 per cent).

A lot of thought has been devoted to the decline of the art of song writing. We have today a brilliant repertoire of first-class art songs by serious composers of many lands, a successful continuation of the traditions set earlier in the century by Richard Strauss, Ravel, Respighi, or De Falla. On the other side of the musical aisle in the popular field, the harvest is, of course, abundant. But it wasn't too long ago—and many of these writers are still alive—that a whole literature of songs was created, standing squarely *between* the high- and the low-brow, songs that were a source of delight and inspiration to millions and a most enjoyable source of revenue to their creators and publishers. Who, today, writes a simple, convincing ballad—such as *Until*, or *Sylvia*, or *Bless This House?* Dozens of these songs were created both here and abroad. In many a year scarcely a secular song of a similar striking power has been added to the rapidly fading list. Radio and its over-exploitation of material, the movies, the hit-parade techniques of our day—everything has been

blamed for the strange paralysis that seems to have overcome the creative power of the men and women who
used to pour out these moving, extremely successful
pieces.

I would rather think that what made the well of their
inspiration dry out is the disappearance of the simple life
they lived and wrote about, of plain, straight faith in God
and his commandments and in the gentle, homespun
things and beliefs that made these songs real and genuine
to those who wrote them and to those who sang them
and listened to them. If you don't believe in a Blessed
House any more, in the simple beauty of Trees, in love
and undisturbed happiness of the heart, how can you sing
about them? . . .

The busiest men in any editorial department, of course,
are the piano editors. There is an occasional sonata, a Set
of Three Pieces, a Suite in the Style of Couperin to
brighten up their days. But these are rare and far-between
morsels. Most of these men feed (by an admirable fund
of mettle, if with a smile that has become bitter and
slightly mad through the years) on a straight daily diet
of elfins, daffodils, sailboats, dwarfs, little beavers, rose
petals, hummingbirds, snowflakes, gremlins, toy soldiers,
Hindu temple bells, little ballerinas, penguins, skating
stars, Chinese jugglers, Panpipes, sleigh rides, wigwam
drums, sunbeam frolics, spring rains, summer nights,
autumn leaves, and winter tales.

The quantities in which this sort of merchandise for

the juvenile trade is produced, printed, and sold defies
the imagination. Fortunes, nay, empires have been built
on the simple fact that millions of children *begin* to
take piano lessons while only a few thousand last long
enough to ever play the *Waldstein Sonata*. It has been
my great privilege to meet, rather intimately, one of these
empire builders, Steve Strode, who made a great fortune
publishing music for the pre-fetus, fetus, and early post-
natal grades. It happened years ago, soon after my arrival
in America, but it made a lasting impression on me and
all the details still stand out clearly in my mind as if it
had happened yesterday—as, in fact, it well might have:
Steve's philosophy, I found out later, is timeless, his
wisdom universal. I can only blame myself for the fact
that our friendship, ultimately, came to nought, and will,
forever, gratefully remember the hours I sat at his feet,
drinking in thirstily the unknown commercial wonders
of the New World. It was through him that I learned the
rudiments of a musical philosophy that made me appreciate, much later, the fact that Beethoven and the
Emigrant Savings Bank are not quite as opposed to each
other as a recent arrival from Vienna might naïvely sup-
pose.

At first our relationship got off to a slow start. Steve
always suspected me of being a high-brow, a state of mind
he considered not only with contempt but with pity. For
quite some time pity took the upper hand, and I felt
bestowed on me the condescending love of a father towards an errant, slightly underprivileged child, a child

that might still be shown the proper ways of life although there is little hope.

He had taken it upon himself to show me how to "become one of the boys." "Unless you become one of the boys," he kept telling me, "you'll never amount to anything in this country." He employed a definite method of education. Every time we met he would bring along a bunch of clippings which he seemed to collect with diabolic industry. The Philadelphia Orchestra went begging for alms, an opera company had folded up somewhere in the wild West, leaving its members stranded on the shores of the Colorado or some other forbidding river. A famous concert singer had canceled an appearance in Carnegie Hall to appear in a movie with Abbott and Costello. It was a great day for Steve when he thrust a clipping at me revealing the fact that a well-known symphonic composer had been discovered working as a waiter in Greenwich Village. "The guy is starving to death," Steve cried triumphantly, and when the Metropolitan Opera issued an appeal for public contributions his exuberance became limitless. "If they don't make money, why don't they close the joint?" he summed up his feelings.

It is easy to imagine that all this shocked me to the roots. Yet Steve was a tremendous success! He had a spacious estate in Commuting County, a magnificent car or three, and when it came to fur coats the missus wouldn't play second mink to nobody. All this he had created with his bare hands and out of the humblest be-

ginnings, and not once in all his life—he proudly and
frequently stressed his record—had he been to Carnegie
Hall. When I once suggested, during the early stages of
our relationship, that he should stay in town for the evening and go with me to the opera, he looked at me with
unbelieving amazement. "I haven't missed that 5.47 in
thirty years," he said with a finality that made me blush.

As if he wanted to emphasize his proud defiance of
anything that happened in the lofty realms of the arts,
Steve maintained a dusty place of business which covered
a whole floor in a district famous more for its garments
than for its melodies. Here he arrived every morning at
eight thirty-four, at a time when other music merchants
were still mumbling happily in Morpheus' or some other
pleasant companion's arms, and would, at once, delve
among his music. Incredible masses of it were stored on
creaking bins, stacked up to the ceiling. Fast as they
multiplied, there were never enough of them. The corridors that separated them became smaller and smaller.
Supporting beams were thrust against every wall and
water pipe, threatening the uninitiated with decapita-
tion. Order fillers had to be picked not for their brains
but for their waistline, and I shall never forget the day
when a man—slightly overweight, I guess, after a week
end in the Catskills—was discovered, after several days,
helplessly trapped between Sacred Octavo, nibbling
thirstily at a copy of At the Waters of Babylon.

But Sacred Octavo meant nothing to Steve. Walking
around among his beloved bins and watching tremen-

dous mountains of music going out on one end of the floor while exhausted printers delivered replacements at the other end, he would, again and again, explain the philosophy that had gotten him where he was.

"Don't you see," I still can hear him expound the sermon he never got tired of delivering, "don't you see: there are millions of kids who start playing an instrument. They don't want to, but somebody, usually a mother, makes them. They don't like it. But they have no defense—yet. So little Dave takes piano lessons. *And as long as that kid plays the piano, somebody has to buy music for him.* See what I mean?"

Sure.

"But soon Dave gets older and stronger and more obstinate, and then the day is here when even that mother can't drag him to the piano no more. He quits. Get it?"

Sure. He quits.

"But now, don't you see what happens?"

Well, Dave quits piano playing. Who cares?

"Who cares? I care. *That boy is lost as a customer forever.* He'll never buy another piece of music in all his life. And there are millions of them. Millions give up after the first year or two. The next year another couple of hundred thousands drop out. And then—what is left? Horowitz!"

He hurled the name at me with a sneering contempt that made me shiver.

"Horowitz," he repeated. "Who wants to publish music for Horowitz? The guy probably don't pay for his music anyway—wants it for free—all you high-brows do. I am not interested in Horowitz. I am interested in Dave —just before he quits. Millions and millions and millions of Daves . . ."

He paused for a moment, staring in space as if overcome by his vision.

"Take, for instance, Rubinstein's *Melody in F*," he continued at last, guiding me across the floor to Bin 1469C and taking out a thin sheet of music. "Now here is a piece that would appeal to millions of children. But it ain't good. It's in F. It has a flat at the beginning of each stave. That's for Horowitz. It ain't for Dave. And yet—I made it a best seller. Here, take a look."

He stepped back, gripped one of the bulbs that were swinging eerily in each corridor and brought it up to make sure I wouldn't miss anything. I opened the music. The title page read: *Rubinstein's famous Melody in F, arranged for the young folks of America by Howard R. Childfiend. A Steve Strode Publication. Our Motto: You, Too, Can Play It Or Your Money Back*. There was no danger of a refund ever being demanded. Childfiend—he was Steve's chief arranger and a writer of volcanic prolificacy—had not only omitted every chord and presented the melody in the nude. He had done much more. The forbidding flat was missing! The last offending association with Horowitz had been removed. Steve's genius became manifest in its full magnitude. He had done what nobody had ever thought of doing before. He had published Rubinstein's *Melody in F* in C!

I would like to dwell in more detail on Steve Strode and his fabulous treasures of Rubinstein-Childfiend, Theme-from-the-Eroica-and-other-Beethoven-lollipops-Childfiend, Bach for little Toots-Childfiend, Everything-underthesun-Childfiend. I am particularly tempted to describe the thirty-five-acre dwelling (Steve, pointing at the gratefully inscribed picture that decorated his office, always called it a château) Childfiend had bought himself with his first royalty check, barely a year after Steve had met him as a thirty-dollar-a-week piano teacher hanging around in a music store in Tennessee. But we have to hurry on. Let me just report then, briefly, an incident that brought our somehow ill-mated relationship to the parting point.

I know today that it was a tactless and quite unnecessary mistake to point out to Steve that something seemed to be wrong with the picture he had chosen for the title page of the Childfiend-DeBussy *Afternoon of a Faun,* one of his wildest sellers. I wasn't criticizing the spelling of Debussy—as long as Childfiend was spelled correctly, who cared. But foolishly I felt it my duty to state that the picture of a *fawn,* surrounded by a mother deer and a paternal stag, all grazing on a very green pasture, didn't quite convey the meaning of the music and its famous title.

Steve became very irritated. "What are you talking about?" he said. "It's green, that's clear enough for afternoon and it's a fawn. So what's the matter?"

"But it's a faun, not a fawn," I said uneasily, writing

both words on a piece of paper. While I handed it to Steve I knew already that I should never have done so.

He looked at the two words for a short moment. Then he spoke.

"I have sold 325,000 copies of this piece of merchandise, and I am making 8½ cents clear profit on every copy. And now you come and try to tell me how to spell. There is nothing the matter with my title page, but there is something the matter with you. I've thought of it for a long time and now I know for sure. You'll never be one of the boys."

16115

Melody

IN F

IN F

Steve, of course, is still around, ruling over his flat-less empire of minks and châteaus, and millions of little Davids still play the harp, smashing it in disgust at the tender age of nine. But the rapidly changing musical climate of America has also rapidly changed the outlook, the responsibility, the business methods, and the scope of the American music publishing industry. It has become a big, important and very mature industry and in the strange tidings that have so heavily affected the balance of musical power throughout the world it has become a factor of importance far beyond its commercial and artistic aspirations here at home.

There are today in the United States more than one hundred so-called Standard Music Publishers—a standard publisher being one who doesn't publish popular music but prints, disseminates, and generally administers classical, educational, serious music—without any regard, of course, for its standard. The most significant feature is the fact that only a handful of them are old houses of established national and international repute. The great majority are very recent arrivals.

Only some twenty years ago one could count the number of American music publishers on the fingers of one and a half hands. There was, of course, the house of G. Schirmer, founded in 1861 by a German immigrant, and I don't think I can do myself much harm by stating that the firm is considered the largest, the most important, and the most prominent member of the guild. But there are other houses of significance and tradition: Carl Fischer, likewise a German colony, started operations in 1872. Two other arrivals from Germany, Joseph and Ignaz Fischer, began to publish music in, of all places, Dayton, Ohio, in 1864 but moved their establishment, J. Fischer & Brother, to New York a few years later. There are similar houses in Philadelphia, Boston, and in New York. Most of these founding fathers were Europeans who had learned the fundamentals of their trade in the old traditional centers of music publishing—Leipzig, Vienna, Amsterdam, London. They brought with them the thoroughness, the sometimes cumbersome traditions, the ancient routine of the profession.

In many of these houses you can still feel real German *Gründlichkeit* (although most of the *Gemütlichkeit* has been crushed in the rush of American life) and a keen sense of tradition that has never been lost, not even in the hectic boom days of vaudeville and the silent movies with their fabulous consumption of second-rate musical fare, still reflected in the catalogues of such houses as Schirmer's or Fischer's through thousands of forever silenced *furiosos, adagio funèbres,* and *prestos* which, for all their hurry, never got anywhere.

There is something old-fashioned about the music publishing business. The presidents of big, powerful establishments might ride around in Cadillacs, live in air-conditioned apartments with deep freezers and built-in television sets, travel in jet-propelled planes and get Frank Lloyd Wright to build them a house in the country and Braque to paint its triangled walls: they still do their work in dark, old leather chairs at fragile, time-stained desks whose mysterious little drawers have not been emptied since 1873. The walls of their offices are covered with faded photographs of bearded grandfathers, top-hatted uncles standing erect on a shaded porch in Elmhurst, photos inscribed by Liszt, Meyerbeer, or Walter Damrosch. No two-way radio, no dictaphone or wire recorder to converse with a slick secretary. Maybe an old buzzer or bell, but usually just the forceful voice of a real man to call in what isn't slick but fits the surroundings.

In the presidential offices of Carl Fischer's or Schirmer's or Gray's in skyscraping New York you could imagine yourself under the shady trees by the sleepy canal at Alsbach's in Amsterdam, or at Schott's in Mainz in the little winding alley where Richard Wagner used to pay stormy visits, or at Durand's, Place de la Madeleine in

Paris, where it looks and smells exactly as it must have looked and smelled when Berlioz, Gounod, Debussy made their calls. It would never surprise me to meet Chopin in one of the corridors at Schirmer's. I would feel out of place. He wouldn't.

Everything connected with the music publishing business is slow, cumbersome, scarcely adaptable to modern methods of production and distribution. In an age where music has been subjected to the streamlined communications of FM radio, LP records, television, tape, and wire, the publisher still operates, basically, as he did when he opened in 1861. Nothing can be hurried. No machines, no electronic devices have replaced the slow, manual methods that were employed in the days of Palestrina and Bach.

To prepare a manuscript for the printer is a painstaking, never-ending job, and no matter how skillful and experienced the editor, he is bound to stumble somewhere in the endless labyrinth of slurs, stems, dots, trills, fermatas, sharps, naturals, and flats. Even more old-fashioned and exasperating is the engraving of the plate, the process equivalent to the setting up of a page of a book in type. There is no equivalent for the linotype machine in music. We are still at the Gutenberg stage.

The unending variety of a musical picture, the delicate spacing, the necessity of laying out a page so that it ends with a bar line, and of planning the engraving of a piece so that the last bar comes at the bottom of a page, the problem of providing suitable turns, the hundred different symbols, lines, tempo and dynamic indications that make up a page of music have never been projected satisfactorily by a machine. There is no typewriter for the composer, no linotype for the printer: everything is done by hand. If an engraver can do three pages of music during a working day he is a fine and accomplished craftsman. It is not only the mechanical labor: the hammering in of each separate note, rest, accent by use of a steel stencil placed carefully on the previously indicated spot, the drawing of slurs by hand, of lines with a ruler, the exasperating work of correcting mistakes by first flattening the indentation and then hammering in the correct item. There is more to it: a great amount of beauty or ugliness, of attractiveness or irritating clumsiness reflects from the engraver's work. He can, virtually, enhance or restrain the beauty of a musical page. He can make the music sing— or just trot along, tired, dull, and pedestrian.

In one respect only—and it is an important one— real progress has been made in the production of music. In the earlier days the engraved plate itself was used for the printing of a musical volume; many a music lover has still in his library some of the lovely old editions where the dedication to His Royal Highness, the Erbprinz of Sachsen-Coburg-Gotha, and the following pages of music faithfully reflect the deep impression made by the metal of the plate on heavy, expensive paper: indestructible footprints of solidity, sturdiness, and wealth. Today, printing is done by the offset press: a photograph is made from a clean proof taken from the engraved plate and imposed on the rubber cylinders of the press which grind out any number of prints. The painstaking labor that goes into the engraving of the plate becomes even more pathetic: like some of the gay little insects that dance in the light just for one day, it has played its part forever. After it has been photographed its usefulness is over.

This turned out to be a development of almost historical importance for the preservation of music's most valuable treasures. Great quantities of plates were destroyed in the holocaust of the last war which hit mercilessly at such venerable places of music publishing as Leipzig, Berlin, Vienna, London, and Milan. Without the miracle of offset printing they would have been irreplaceable. Today, even such grievous losses do not matter. As long as there was a single copy of the printed music left anywhere in the world, no plates were needed to reproduce it. The photographic lens and the rubber cylinders of the offset press could duplicate the original in any desired quantities.

These, however, were not the only blessings bestowed on music by modern printing devices. The volcanic development of the American music publishing industry would be unthinkable without the photographic reproduction of hundreds of thousands of pages of music! When a prominent Austrian publisher recently paid a visit to a prominent American colleague, his host asked him, politely, whether he would like to see his printing plant—his *Druckerei.* "*Sie meinen wohl Ihre Nach-druckerei*," said the visitor, not without bitterness referring to the magnificent, busy factory as to a *re-printery.*

He had a good point there. An amazing variety of music is now being printed—in many cases reprinted, photographed from European editions—in this country. More and more the American music consumer becomes independent of European imports, more and more American musical demands can be satisfied from domestic sources. American music publishing has become an important, responsible industry, not only providing for the needs of a swiftly expanding market at home but already exporting many of its products all over the world, even into Europe itself, which, only a few decades ago, seemed to hold an unbreakable monopoly on the creation of musical properties.

It was a development born out of necessity. As the demands for every kind of printed music increased all over the United States in a rapid, steady pace, the accustomed European sources of supply began to dry out. The process had already begun during the early Hitler years with their economic, artistic, and moral upheaval. It became an acute crisis when the last war cut off even the slightest trickle of supplies. Soon it became a matter of starvation or self-sufficiency. The mighty tool of the offset press, slightly aided by the alien property custodian, who seized and made available many foreign properties, and by the U. S. Copyright Law, which puts a minimum of restrictions in the path of such sweeping activities, helped a new development that has now become of great importance to the musical progress of America.

Hundreds of scores and orchestral parts of the classical standard repertoire—Beethoven, Haydn, Mozart, Brahms, Tchaikovsky, Rimsky-Korsakov, César Franck, even Johann Strauss and Offenbach—have now been published here. Fine original editions happily replace the cheap commercial arrangements of classical masterpieces that have been an embarrassing American specialty, corrupting the musical taste of a whole generation during the earlier, the darker ages of American music publishing. Chamber music, oratorios, songs, every conceivable piano piece from Buxtehude to Bartók is available in fine, clean, and up-to-date prints. You can choose between many editions of the Beethoven Sonatas, the Bach *Well-Tempered Clavier*, the Mozart String Quartets, the songs by Schubert, Brahms, or Richard Strauss. You can buy the full orchestral scores of *Figaro*, *Carmen*, *Faust*, or *Pagliacci*, of the Bach Cantatas, the Mozart Piano Concertos, the Verdi *Requiem*. There is sharp, relentless competition, and it's all to the best for the cause of music. Quality of print and, more important, quality of musical fidelity are steadily improving. Only the finest editions can survive.

A publisher in Ann Arbor has even begun to reprint the innumerable extensive and expensive volumes of the famous *Gesamt Ausgabe* of the complete works by J. S. Bach, Beethoven, Brahms, Mozart, and other masters, huge tomes of thousands and thousands of pages, once published in Leipzig and Vienna, but out of print and lost to the world for many years. When the Bach edition was first offered for subscription in 1851, 553 subscribers signed up in Europe, only 17 in the United States. Today this vast collection of musical treasures carries the revealing and significant imprint "Made in U.S.A."

To make the picture even more colorful and attractive, famous European publishers have now established their own branches in America or have associated themselves with an American house. The list is impressive and clearly indicative of the new fortunes of music in the world. Breitkopf & Haertel (who now have two branches in Germany—one in Leipzig, behind, and one in Wiesbaden, this side of the Iron Curtain), Schott Söhne of Mainz, C. F. Peters (also torn in pieces by the political separation of Germany), and Eulenburg (the famous yellow pocket scores!) now print the bulk of their publications, once the pride of the German industry, here in America. Salabert, Durand et Fils, and Heugel of Paris; Oxford Press, Curwen, and Boosey & Hawkes of England; Ricordi of Italy; Wilhelm Hansen of Copenhagen, each one of them known to music consumers all over the world, now make their editions directly available to the American market. And when I need any of the publications of Universal Edition, many of which I helped to publish myself during the fifteen years I worked for them in Vienna, I can get them right across the street—Berg's *Wozzeck*, for instance, Schönberg's *Gurrelieder*, *Schwanda*, or *Dreigro-*

schenoper, and many more of the nostalgic and wonderful memories of a former life. . . .

There is one more participant in the impressive parade —a humble, modest, slightly embarrassed man who usually comes in through the back door if he is admitted at all: the contemporary American composer. A few years ago it was but a brazen dream for a member of the longhaired fraternity to expect his music to be published in his own country. Wealthy patrons stepped in to finance a few scattered publications; many of the earlier works of some of our most famous composers were printed in the Cos Cob Press, called after the estate of the bighearted lady who made these publications—a simple act of charity —possible.

That, of course, wasn't sufficient. Composers banded together in co-operatives, paying themselves not only for the publication but for the administration of their printed works. The catalogue of Arrow Press, founded in 1938 by some fifty composers, still contains many of the earlier and some of the most successful works of such recognized leaders of American music as Aaron Copland, Walter Piston, Virgil Thomson, Roy Harris, and William Schuman. Henry Cowell was responsible for still another gimmick—a quarterly publication called New Music in which he published (and still publishes) "new compositions which might not have a chance of distribution through ordinary channels." New Music, too, is a non-profit membership co-operative, limiting itself to music for piano, voice, and small ensembles. It has done a fine job. Such unusual and highly experimental composers as John J. Becker, Paul Bowles (before he became a successful writer of novels and short stories), Carlos Chavez of Mexico, Carl Ruggles, Charles Ives, Edgar Varèse, and John Cage, the man who composes for fourteen radios or, at least, for "prepared piano"—that is, a piano that is made to sound *not* like a piano by sticking pieces of wood, glass, steel, wool, rubber, rock, or a finger or two between its strings. If you are interested in an Ionization for chamber orchestra, a Mirrorrorrim for piano, an auto accident for percussion, or a work called *Only Themselves Understand Themselves*, get New Music! Your troubles are over.

Today many American composers have found permanent associations with commercial publishers here at home. Their music is printed, their scores are properly distributed to orchestras, radio stations, ballet companies, performing artists, and opera houses. Agencies of the leading American publishers in Europe, South America, or Australia help towards world-wide recognition of new American music. Even a few of the big boys in the popular field have begun serious flirtations with such questionable amours as symphonies and cello sonatas.

From time to time one can see a genuine high-brow composer sneak uneasily into the Brill Building or some similar house of ill repute, hiding a score of a *Sonata Serena* or, God forbid, a *Triple Fugue for Strings, Percussion, and Solo Bassoon* under a shabby raincoat.

We have come a long way. Strip-teasers help to finance

the publication of twelve tone concertos, and the boys at the Taft Hotel have to try out symphonies before they are allowed to begin the Beguine.

It sounds wonderful.

Almost too good to be true.

Sonata

SERENA

This morning, on my way to work, before the paper was ground to dust in the millstones of the shuttle train, I was reading about John Steinbeck. Or was it Hemingway or Irwin Shaw or Thornton Wilder? It was, in any case, an American writer of artistic integrity, public recognition, genuine talent, and cultural significance. It could have been any of them or of a dozen others, similarly prominent, established, and successful. It said there that the man's new novel had sold half a million copies.

I was very much interested. All my life I have been associated with just that type of people: writers of artistic integrity, public recognition, genuine talent, cultural significance: Béla Bartók, for instance, Arnold Schönberg, Copland, or Samuel Barber: the Hemingways, the Shaws, the Wilders of music. And now it said in the paper that the book had sold half a million copies.

Many, I figured, were probably book-club specials, selling at reduced prices and yielding a reduced royalty to the writer. Others might have been cheap pocket editions— and perhaps the figure was altogether a little on the optimistic side. But no matter how I looked at it, the writer must have culled a soothing $100,000 from the sales of copies of his book alone. And there were, in addition, the possible and most likely sale of the movie rights (anything between $75,000 and a quarter of a million), serialization in magazines, translations into Turkish and Sanskrit, condensations, dramatizations on radio and television, or the transformation of the story into a Broadway musical—every one of these uses certain to unleash still another torrent of cash on the author and—I am only human, after all—on his publisher as well.

And now I find here on my desk a memo from the Publication Department, stating with pride and visible satisfaction that a new piano sonata, published last year, has just gone into its second print of one thousand copies. This, they say, will last for the rest of the year, but they are confident that a third print will be forthcoming "in due course."

It isn't just any old piano sonata. It is the *Sonata Serena* by Gibner Irmigstad, one of America's most important composers, a famous man, known and respected all over the world, equal if not superior as a serious writer to the author of the gold-sputtering novel. The novel, at its appearance on the scene, had been greeted by rave notices. So had the sonata, which also won the Critics Award, the

Naumburg Citation, and the Alice B. Guggensteiner Medal and was brilliantly premièred in Carnegie Hall by Amir Rubevitz, the world-famous pianist who, afterwards, played it all over America, Europe, and Central Honduras, and also recorded it for a world-famous recording company which announced that it was proud to announce it.

The copies of the *Sonata Serena* eventually sold (and I'll double the Publication Department's gloomy optimism and boldly predict a staggering sale of six thousand) will yield the composer not $100,000, not $10,000, but $1,500, spread over fifteen years, in royalties, or—get this, Steinbeck—approximately two dollars a week.

He can't get fat on that, can he? Now what about the performances in Carnegie Hall and similar temples of the muse, each one, of course, sold out to the rafters at the mere whispering of Rubevitz' name? When Rubevitz played in Carnegie Hall he paid, gladly and without batting an eyelash:

Rental of Carnegie Hall	$750.00
Ushers	150.00
Box Office and Tickets	75.00
Manager	200.00
Tuning and Carting of Piano	55.00
Advertising	300.00
Posters and Window Cards	57.50
	$1,587.50

He also paid, after having batted a most indignant eyelash, the amount of $15 (fifteen dollars) to ASCAP, the

American Society of Composers, Authors and Publishers. For this amount he has the right to play on his recital as many pieces of copyright music as he pleases, be they announced on his printed program or thrown in as an encore. Every time he breaks out in the *Ritual Fire Dance* or one of his little war ponies by Ravel, I sit on needles as the fifteen dollars get stretched out thinner and thinner. By the time ASCAP divides them among all the composers, heirs of the deceased, arrangers, publishers here and abroad, agents and representatives, each one will get something in the neighborhood of seventy-five cents. The total take at Carnegie Hall, that night, had been $7,600.

The composer will have to wait for his seventy-five cents till the next ASCAP accounting comes around, sometime next year. In the meantime he is, of course, expected to attend the concert in a newly pressed suit, a freshly laundered shirt, and spotlessly shined shoes. If he doesn't show up and come backstage afterwards to kiss the hand of the pianist, out goes the *Sonata Serena* and the next time Stravinsky will make the seventy-five cents.

Gibner Irmigstad should consider himself fortunate at that. That there is any remuneration paid for the public performance of a work is a rather recent development. For centuries all the law would give the composer was a somehow shaky protection against actual pirating—that is, reprinting—of his published music. That a public performance for profit should be the composer's exclusive property, illegal unless he has given his consent, appeared on the American lawbooks only as late as 1897. Even then it was a right that existed solely on paper. How could a composer enforce it?

No one could roam the land, arrest a string quartet at Luchow's, or hand a summons to a dance-hall proprietor in San Francisco. Thousands of "music users"—orchestras, minstrel shows, town bands, hotels, concert artists— just kept playing and singing and making money. Nobody paid attention to the new law as long as there was nobody to enforce it. For seventeen years after the new law had been passed, not a single instance is known of a composer collecting a penny for the public exploitation of his music.

Then, in 1914, a group of composers, writers, and publishers, led by Victor Herbert and John Philip Sousa, got together in an attempt to translate the pale words of the law into practical life. They organized ASCAP and began to license hotels, cabarets, vaudeville entrepreneurs, dance halls, and movie theaters. For seven torturous years expenses devoured the slowly trickling income. No royalties were paid to the members. Then, with a terrific, wonderful bang, radio arrived on the scene.

Today, ASCAP represents the combined musical properties of more than two thousand composers and writers and nearly three hundred and fifty music publishers. It also puts at the disposal of its subscribers, whose most important group are America's 1,051 radio stations and rapidly growing network of television stations, the works of some fifty thousand foreign composers and writers, administered in the United States through ASCAP, which has mutual agreements with many similar organizations throughout the world. ASCAP has been battled in the courts, it has been outlawed in a few states of the Union, it has been attacked as a trust and rival societies have been organized. It is still a big, powerful, most important symbol of American musical maturity, collecting and passing on to its members, after its own expenses have been paid, more than fourteen million dollars each year.

The composer of the *Sonata Serena*, while waiting for his seventy-five cents to arrive from ASCAP and wondering who gets the remaining $13,999,999.25, should not feel too bitter. He should be happy in the thought that mighty ASCAP has gotten around at all to paying even the slightest attention to a character like him. For decades past, the deafening roar of the millions, propelled into ASCAP's bulging coffers by their vast repertoire of popular music, completely outroared the miserable cries of the long-haired beggars at their doors. Now Gibner can at least sit down and read one of ASCAP's beautifully (and expensively) gotten up pamphlets, written especially for him.

"It has been a criticism of the music field for years that the writer of serious musical literature has found it impossible to earn a livelihood from his compositions," he will read with a deep feeling of gratitude and relief. "Sales of sheet music are limited, and the income therefrom negligible. Nor does the sale of symphonic material provide adequate income."

Here the writer of serious musical literature will stop and wonder who drafts ASCAP's beautiful pamphlets and whether they couldn't have found *someone* among their two thousand writers who could have helped them out, even if the income therefrom is negligible. But obviously they didn't and so he reads on:

"This situation has forced the majority of serious composers, no matter how brilliant and successful, into other fields such as teaching and radio. When it is remembered that these composers produce much of the musical literature which interprets the American scene for the rest of the world such diversion of talent becomes tragic. It is the Society's object to stimulate the productivity of these creators by providing through its licensing policy the financial encouragement which will obviate the necessity of their making a living outside of their profession."

At this point the ardent reader is interrupted. An armored truck, on its way to deliver twenty-one heavy royalty bags to the creator of *On Top of Old Smoky*, stops, the driver leans out and hands Gibner Irmigstad his seventy-five cents, thus stimulating the productivity of the creator by providing the financial encouragement which will obviate the necessity of his making a living.

ASCAP means well. The fifteen dollars they have extracted from Rubevitz, and similar crumbs they begin to collect on the dusty fields of serious music, are the results of long and bitter battles. They are the first timid token of victories over the combined forces of the concert world who think nothing of sending a private piano tuner from

New York to San Francisco to get Mr. Rubevitz' piano in shape, who squander thousands upon thousands on personal representatives, press agents, and pictures of baby-kissing conductors or Hungarian pianists being admitted to the venerable tribe of the Blackfeet by Chief Heavy Thumb, but who will scream in outright indignation when asked to pay more than a ridiculous and shameful alm to the men who stand at the very base of all their doing, scheming, and money-making, and without whom there would be neither music nor music business —the contemporary composer.

There can be no doubt that Mrs. Anna O'Dougal née Himmelstoss, a scrubwoman, although undoubtedly a master of her craft, takes more money out of Carnegie Hall than Aaron Copland, Samuel Barber, and Roy Harris combined. The Boston Symphony Orchestra, whose box-office receipts exceed $1,000,000 per year (and that doesn't include the additional income of $160,000 from record royalties), pays $789,839 to its players, conductors, and soloists but only $3,000 to ASCAP, less than 0.3 per cent of the receipts for the use of copyright music in 230 concerts in Boston, on tour, at the Pops, the Esplanade, and the Berkshires, an average of $13 per concert. If the orchestra should operate in France, for example, it would pay 4.4 per cent of its gross receipts for music of contemporary composers—$44,000 instead of $3,000. As for Rubevitz, he really gets away with murder. He who so grudgingly pays $15 for the use of ASCAP repertory in Carnegie Hall is assessed 6.6 per cent of the receipts in France—$500 instead of $15! And there is no kidding about it, either. The agents of the French ASCAP, dignified but determined messieurs in tuxedos, sit right in the box office and take away the loot before Rubevitz can set out for points west. Similar conditions prevail in Italy, Spain, Switzerland, Austria, Germany, and England, and in Iceland there are most frigid rules about it.

Where else should the contemporary composer look for support? Hollywood, the commercial pictures look like a logical field for him to earn a dishonest penny. But are they? Most decidedly, they are not. Of the top-notch contemporary composers only—but here comes Miss Bishop with a telegram that seems to need immediate attention. Next to Beethoven and Miss Love, Miss Bishop is the prime asset of this office. She loves to work in a music publishing house. The sight of a conductor walking across the balcony fills her with joy, and as long as Gian-Carlo Menotti greets her once in a while with a rrrollling Heelloooow she'll never ask for a raise, which is only for the best. She works in the high-brow department. Material gains must never be her goal. She has to feel rewarded by the great and wonderful sensation that she once shook hands with Eugene Ormandy.

The telegram comes from the conductor of the Columbus Symphony, who wants to see, urgently, the score of Gibner Irmigstad's new symphony. Miss Bishop, that lovely marvel of all marvels, brings not only the telegram.

She also brings the score of the symphony. It is a beautiful copy, 187 pages at ten dollars a page, union rate, just paid for by us, and Miss Bishop carries it as if it were the Holy Grail.

"Isn't it wonderful!" she says. She isn't referring to Mr. Irmigstad's symphony. She is referring to the telegram from Columbus.

We (she, that is) had written letters to every conductor in the country, had enclosed extracts from press reviews and a biographical sketch of the composer—and now Vudricek in Columbus asks for it. Miss Bishop is all smiles.

I am not. Miss Bishop is young. I am a little older. Miss Bishop is looking forward to life's wonderful surprises. I am looking back on life's soul-clearing disappointments. Miss Bishop does not know what will happen in Columbus. I do.

Vudricek will get the score, will read through it, will decide that he has to do something sometimes for a native and will put it on his program. The manager of the orchestra will write to us, asking for terms for the loan of score and parts "for a pair of concerts in February."

As it happens, in the same mail he will write to Mr. Solar Jurock, the concert manager, in New York. He wants the great Rubevitz to play the Tchaikovsky concerto on the same program.

The answers will arrive a few days later. One comes from the secretary to the secretary to Mr. Jurock. Rubevitz is terribly busy. However, in view of our old, we may.

The fee is at present $4,000; however, in view of, it might be soon. We request, therefore, that you immediately. Sincerely.

The manager rushes to the next Western Union office. OK Rubevitz and many thanks. Devotedly.

When he comes back to his office he sees the second letter. "I am delighted to know of your and Mr. Vudricek's interest in Gibner Irmigstad's great symphony," I write. "You may be assured that the music will be sent in plenty of time for rehearsals. We are putting two proofreaders on the job to make sure that Mr. Vudricek will have no troubles, no troubles whatsoever, when preparing the performance. We surely appreciate. Very, very, very sincerely yours.

"P.S. May we suggest a fee of $100 to cover the rental of the music for the pair of concerts."

The manager purples with rage. He calls Vudricek, ordering him to remove the symphony from his program at once, "who wants to hear it anyway." Vudricek, purple with rage, calls the composer. The composer, purple, calls me: I have not only clumsily jeopardized an all-important performance but also his lifelong friendship with Vudricek.

In the end, the manager will pay $40 for two performances of the symphony. Gibner will get half, we will get the other half. The copyist's bill came to $1,257.89. The proofreaders don't count. They are on the payroll.

All this is not known to Miss Bishop, who now leaves the office, Irmigstad's score happily pressed against one of the most beautiful busts in the music business. The door closes behind her. All that is left is a wisp of Chanel that makes Major out there circle around his lovable companion in a sudden outburst of tenderness. How nice to be a bird.

Well, I might as well return to the thoughts that were so pleasantly interrupted by Miss Bishop's radiant appearance. Hollywood, I was saying I believe, Hollywood and the commercial pictures seem a logical field for the contemporary composer to earn an occasional penny—but they aren't. The fact of the matter is that Gibner Irmigstad has never been in Hollywood and the chances are, he never will be.

Of the top-notch contemporary composers only Aaron Copland has been able to penetrate behind the golden curtain with a certain amount of regularity—and to return alive. After starting out, as does every Gibner, in the exciting but unprofitable realm of the documentary film with his celebrated score for *The City*, Copland has written the music to such successful pictures as *Of Mice and Men*, *Our Town*, *North Star*, *Red Pony*, and *The Heiress*, which even won him an Oscar. Another composer of serious music, George Antheil, has settled in Hollywood and is allowed an occasional nibble at the less tasty extremities of the golden calf. David Diamond and Darius Milhaud have been brought in for one picture each—and have never been asked again. Ernst Toch and Alexandre Tansman gave up in disgust. Stravinsky, Krenek, and the late

Arnold Schönberg, residents of Hollywood, have never made a picture there. The Polish composer Karol Rathaus, who wrote brilliant music to many German and French films for discriminating producers and directors and was famous for his particular skill in writing this type of film music all over Europe before he came to this country, has never been admitted. Such outstanding figures in American music as Samuel Barber, William Schuman, Walter Piston, Roy Harris, or Norman dello Joio and scores of others, masters in their craft, have been ignored.

Most illuminating is the case of Virgil Thomson, one of the most brilliant and versatile minds in American music. While he might be (and decidedly is) a controversial figure when it comes to concert music and operas (anyone setting Gertrude Stein libretti to music is leading with his chin), the music he has written for several documentary films is anything but controversial: it is striking, beautiful, and highly successful—in a quite straight, popular sense of the word. Two of the scores—the music he wrote for the Pare Lorentz film *The Plough That Broke the Plains* and his score to Robert Flaherty's *Louisiana Story*—have been translated from the screen to the concert stage and have been played by many symphony orchestras and dozens of high-school bands. *Louisiana Story* won the Pulitzer Prize for its composer—it has been recorded, published, and what not—but it has not resulted in a call from MGM.

There is a strange frustration on both sides of the curtain that separates the large group of Hollywood composers from the Irmigstads who make their living as professors, music critics, conductors, orchestra players, businessmen, organists, slaves in a music publishing house, or—shades of Steven Strode!—waiters in Greenwich Village, or write their works on commissions from fiddlers, dancers, or the Louisville Philharmonic Orchestra. It isn't only that the symphonic composer would like to write music for the movies: the closed corporation of Hollywood composers who turn out their dreary bits of background illustration for years on end are just as anxious to break out of their golden cage—and just as unsuccessful. They write sinfoniettas and concertos, they hire orchestras in New York and Oslo to prove to themselves and to the world that they are musicians of artistic integrity, they compose operas and have them produced—but it all is of little avail. Once they are in, the doors of the golden cage stay locked. They cannot write, with one hand, music that pleases the hucksters and with the other hand music that pleases the heart of man. A strange, expensive, and very tasty poison has paralyzed their creative independence. There just seems no way back.

Gibner Irmigstad may as well forget Hollywood. But there still is the recording of the *Sonata Serena*, played by Rubevitz for the world-famous recording company who were so proud to announce it. Here, at least, should be a delectable source of monetary reward for the composer. This is canned music's golden age. How can he fail to get some of the gold? Well, he can and does.

It looks good on the surface. In the few years since the miraculous microgroove, the 33⅓ R(otations) P(er) M(inute) LP record, raised its timid voice, a new, rich world of music has been created.

A few years ago one could count the number of recording companies on the fingers of one hand. Today more than one hundred of them, answering to such new and intriguing names as Oceanic, Esoteric, Dial, Polymusic, Sounds of Our Time, Vanguard, Paradox, and—maybe a little optimistically—Eterna, are busily engaged in building up a repertory of amazing depth and variety. Most of them stick to serious music, leaving the popular field to the well-entrenched big shots.

They go to Europe to record operatic performances, whole oratorios, symphonies, church choirs, ancient madrigals, and contemporary experiments at a fraction of the cost which made the old recordings on wax, loaded as they were with technical problems and prohibitive American union rates, unobtainable to any but the few rich combines. To the miracle of the microgroove has been added the miracle of recording on tape. There is no surface noise, no needle hiss. You can cut in whenever you want, can cut off—with an ordinary pair of scissors—what you don't like, patch in a new note, a new bar, or a whole section of music. Fidelity of the oversensitive magnet is superior to the long-drawn-out trip the sound used to make from the microphone to the needle to the master and then back to the final pressing.

The speed and magnitude of the new development in

recordings of serious music, so vital in this decisive era in American musical history, is amazing. Between sixty and one hundred new titles are added every month to the already fabulous list of available treasures. Some of the companies specialize in the works of the great masters, surprised themselves by the response. The Haydn Society of Boston, for example, started out to sponsor a scholarly edition of the works of the world's most famous Papa—masses, operas, symphonies, concerti, and a complete series of Haydn's eighty-three string quartets—only to discover that there was nothing to sponsor: they were suddenly in business, hastily adding additional gems, such as complete recordings of Mozart's *Don Giovanni* and *Idomeneo*, to their blossoming catalogues—just one more of many examples to prove that the American public is deeply and consistently underrated in its demands for quality. Sales are plentiful. The Budapest Quartet, for instance, has quadrupled the sales of their records since the advent of LP.

Other companies offer complete operas, many quite off the beaten path, such as Puccini's *Turandot*, Verdi's *Ernani*, Rossini's *Cenerentola*, or Strauss's *Elektra*. Still others record folk music from all over the world, medieval and renaissance music, Gregorian chant and modern music. Never before have such riches been offered to musical education, entertainment, and just simple enjoyment.

The contemporary composer, too, has suddenly been showered with unexpected, still a little staggering, attention. There are companies specializing in the most un-compromising works of Schönberg, Bartók, Berg, Messiaen, or Webern. Every European piece of contemporary significance has been released. Lately even the American composer has been allowed to enter the magic circle. Almost every work of Aaron Copland's has been recorded. In a single winter not less than eight of Samuel Barber's compositions have been brought out by five different companies. Schuman, Sessions, Diamond, Thomson—there is no end to the roll call.

It's wonderful, and yet it is tragic. At this point, and just when the composer could rightly feel that he was somewhere, somehow coming into his own, the Law itself, the American copyright law, steps in in all its might and majesty to cut him down again to his proper size. Recording companies may flourish, artists and orchestras may get their full share, dealers may make profits and disk jockeys enjoy the dawn of a new age. The composer, and he alone, is prohibited by law from fully taking his place in the breadline. Everybody, the law says, may make money but Tchaikovsky.

The law, passed in 1909, in the days of hand-propelled victrolas, piano rolls, free luncheons, and nickel cigars, and before radio, juke boxes, electrical transcriptions, wire recorders, sound film, television—the whole arsenal of present and future mechanical exploitation of music—were ever thought of, the law stipulates a fee of two cents as royalty for the composer for the use of his work on "mechanical devices." There is no bargaining, no free enterprise—there is even the "compulsory license": after you have given one company the right to record your work, anyone else, paying you the two cents under the law, can record it too. You can't grant anyone an exclusive; you can't plead that the cost of living went up a bit since 1909—it's two cents, take it or leave it. You take it, of course.

But that isn't all. When the law was passed there was no LP in existence. A side of a record, priced at two cents by the law, contained not more than four minutes of music, at its best. Now the *Sonata Serena*, playing twenty-four minutes, appears on *one* side—on one single side—of an LP record. The law says . . .

You can figure out the rest for yourself.

Well, there it is, Steinbeck. Be a nice fellow: take Gibner across the street and buy him a lunch at Sacher's. You can afford it. And get a bottle of wine with it. Let him drink to ASCAP, Rubevitz, MGM, Oceanic Records, and to the American Copyright Law. I'll join you in a little while—and the round of drinks that goes to Copyright will be on me. I'll even give you a little speech with it.

Go ahead in the meantime. I'll be right over. I have to attend to important business first. Don't you see the smile of transfiguration on Miss Bishop's radiant face? That can only mean one thing: Vudricek has arrived from Columbus, Ohio—or, if it isn't Vudricek, one of his one hundred fifty distinguished colleagues.

None of my days would be perfect without a visit with a symphonic conductor.

A FRANK AND UNRESTRAINED
REPORT ON THE AUTHOR'S
LIFELONG CONTACTS WITH
AND IMPRESSIONS OF
SYMPHONIC CONDUCTORS HERE
AND ABROAD

Shortly after Charles O'Connell had published his celebrated book *The Other Side
of the Record*, a frank and unrestrained report on the author's lifelong contacts with
and impressions of symphonic conductors
here and abroad, he made the following
statement to the press: "I think I have written myself out of the music business."

I'd like to stay in it.

End of Chapter.

LUNCHEON
AT
SACHER'S

Many a well-meaning friend has warned me never to use the word copyright in a book. It puts the reader to sleep and he may never wake up again. It tastes, even before you have finished pronouncing it, like stale Saratoga Sprudel.

I once thought so myself. But I know better today. Copyright is not a dull, monotonous spa, populated by goutish lawyers in creaking wheel chairs, discussing the case of Melody Murder Inc. vs. Wrong Key Malone with endless, spirited relish. It rather resembles a wild, flowery jungle teeming with beautiful beasts, lovely parasites, and killers who mercilessly devour those who have no weapons to defend themselves. There are strange mirages on its treacherous lakes, and once in a while you come across a lovers' lane where you hear villainous music publishers whisper sweet words of love into the rosy ears of naïve widows.

That's the way I learned to look at copyright early in life, at the very dawn of my professional career in the business, many, many years ago in Vienna, when I took part in my first hunting expedition into the fabulous wilds of copyright and came home, at night, loaded with cadavers, to feast on roasted pig, fried monkeys, and the delicious tongues of forever silenced nightingales.

The scene was Vienna, the place the music publishing house of Universal Editions, the time 10 A.M. Mr. Winter, vice-president and treasurer, opened the morning mail. Somewhere along the line he came across a simple, open postcard, marked Leipzig, Germany:

> Gentlemen, I would like to use a few bars from the Waltz Song *Lilies of the Valley* in a composition which I am about to publish. I understand that you are the copyright owners in the song. May I have your permission.
>
> Otto Kunze, Music Publisher, Leipzig

Winter had never heard of the song before. He put me on the job, and before night began to fall I had tracked it down. It had been published, years ago, by a small Viennese house which we had purchased recently, lock, barrel, and stock. The sole reason for the transaction had been a famous Austrian march in their catalogue whose acquisition seemed worth the price for all the worthless junk that went with it. Nobody had ever bothered to look through the catalogue. Somewhere between *Roses of the Alps* and *Brookdale Violets* the *Lilies of the Valley* had slumbered quietly and undisturbed.

Herr Winter dictated a letter to Otto Kunze. Glad to oblige, permission granted, fee will be twenty-five dollars. Thank you, sincerely. Then he left. It was four in the afternoon, time for *Kaffee* and *Kuchen*.

There has never been a more profitable cup of afternoon *Klatsch*, a cheaper piece of Sachertorte with cream than the ones that delayed the dispatch of the letter to Kunze for one fateful day. The next morning Treasurer Winter, glancing through the array of complaints, lawsuits, useless manuscripts, personal invectives, and notifications of bankruptcy which had come in with the morning mail, the accustomed bread and butter of the music business, stiffened suddenly as he came across the following letter:

> Gentlemen, If we are not mistaken you are the copyright owners of an old waltz, *Lilies of the Valley*. We consider purchasing the rights of this little song, provided you will quote us a nominal fee. May we hear from you?
>
> > Sincerely
> > Frobenius, Hagestolz and Ehrenreich
> > Music Publishers, Berlin

Treasurer Winter walked over to where the girl had just typed out the letter to Kunze in Leipzig, tore it up carefully, and went down the corridor towards the directors' room where Emil Hertzka, the big, great, unforgettable boss, presided.

Soon a messager was on his hurried way to the stockroom for a copy of *Lilies of the Valley*. He returned empty-handed. The song, he reported, had been out of print for years. There wasn't a single copy around. The printing plates had been melted down.

By now everybody in the place knew that something out of the ordinary was cooking. *Lilies of the Valley*, however, no matter how many of us were racking their eager brains, existed only in the abstract realm of copyright! We owned it, but we didn't have it. Nobody had ever heard it. Nobody remembered it. Someone dug up the contract with the composer: it was all in order, whereas, whereas, now therefore, set my seal. Witnessed Mitzi Vogelsang. Everything was fine. Nothing was missing but the song.

Calls to secondhand music stores, to members of the Home for Old Musicians, to collectors of musical oddities were unavailing. By now the boss filled the corridors with the terrible echoes of his outcries. Men began to congregate in corners, reading the Help Wanted ads.

At last a stock clerk, who at night doubled as a singer in a Schraml Quartet, broke the deadlock. He had spread word through the Schraml world—a world of queer old characters, of zithers and fiddles, voices and sobs, drenched by wine and flavored by salami—and, after a few days of unbearable tension, came happily forward with a copy of the precious song. He handed it to the boss, who acknowledged it with a smile of thanks that sent him staggering back to the stockroom.

The boss picked up the phone and asked to be connected, at once, with Herr Busch, our ambassador to Leipzig, the German musical capital.

"Do you know the song *Lilies of the Valley?*" the boss asked him before the ambassador had been able to get in a *Guten Morgen, Herr Generaldirektor.*

Busch had never heard of it.

"Hold the wire and listen carefully," the boss commanded. A piano player who had been standing by nervously began pounding the song. The boss was holding the receiver inside the old upright. The din must have busted old Busch's distant ears. Suddenly a cry, clearly audible all the way from Leipzig, made the pianist jump off his stool and stop.

"*Um Himmelswillen,*" we heard Busch gasp. "That's the biggest hit in Germany. What do you mean *Lilies of the Valley?* It's called *Trink, Trink, Brüderlein, Trink.* I only wish we owned it."

"We do," said the boss. "Make reservations for me at the Grand Hotel and meet me at the station tomorrow morning."

He got up violently, stuffed the copy of the song in one of his bulging pockets, shouted for someone to get him a berth on the night train, and left.

I did not know that he had returned till, a few days later, the buzzer over the door to my office began to explode. When I rushed out, the place was bedlam. From every office came the rattling of buzzers and bells—we called them His Master's Voice—and I saw Herr Direktor Winter and half a dozen others rushing towards the boss's abode.

As I entered he was leaning over his desk, the whole

length of his arm pressed on the wooden contraption that held all the buttons. He was pressing them all at once. As he saw us, he straightened up. Silence, even more frightening than the deafening bell chorus, descended.

The boss walked over to the big conference table, usually covered with scores, files, inkwells, ash trays, glasses, hats, and many coffee cups. Now it was empty. Everything had been brushed off, piled up on the floor in a wild, careless mess. The table, for some unknown, disquieting reason, was bare.

The boss sat down. Everybody scrambled for chairs. The silence began to tell.

"I thought you gentlemen might be interested in the results of my trip to Germany," he said at last. There was an immediate murmur of relief, little cadences of Yes Sir, But certainly, *Danke schön, Herr Direktor*—but he cut us short with an impatient gesture and continued:

"Will Herr Winter please step over here and take his seat next to me. As treasurer of the company, I want him to give me his full attention."

He put his hand in his left pocket and brought out a little package wrapped in a torn German newspaper. He opened it slowly. There was a gasp and somebody, noisily, broke a doodling pencil. We looked at a small mountain of money.

"Otto Kunze, Leipzig," the boss said. "Fifty-five hundred mark. Please count and make a note."

Winter took the money with trembling fingers and began to count.

"Fifty-five hundred," he said at last. In the meantime Hertzka's hand had returned from a second pocket.

"Siegfried Rubezahl," he said. "Eighty-seven hundred and fifty mark."

The room had fallen into silence. There was only the rustling of the bank notes, the counting, the monotonous responsory of names as Hertzka continued to ransack his garments. He had two outside and two inside pockets in his coat, four in his trousers, and a large one in the tail of his jacket. He even produced a stack of bills from the lining of his hat.

There was also a pocket in the inside of his velvet vest, a fact that surprised everybody and caused, for the first time, a slight stir among the assembly as it suddenly yielded a stack of brand-new thousand-mark notes.

"Frobenius, Hagestolz, and Ehrenreich, twenty-five thousand mark," Hertzka said. It was all over.

"Seventy-eight thousand mark," Winter said, with a heavily veiled voice, and the boss said, "Check," and broke out in a broad, boyish, unbossy smile. Then he told his story.

When he had arrived in Leipzig, the efficient Busch had already ascertained a few basic facts. Wilhelm Lindemann, a singer in a Berlin cabaret, had written a song *Trink, Trink, Brüderlein, Trink,* had performed it to the delight of his audiences, and printed a few thousand copies. It spread like the plague. Lindemann, not equipped to cope with the avalanche of unexpected success, sold printing rights to any publisher who asked for them. A few had gotten suspicious. They had investigated, had discovered that Lindemann had taken his melody bar for bar from the forgotten *Lilies of the Valley*, and had dispatched their harmless little messages to us as the copyright owners. They were good, law-abiding, honest people. Their punishment was immediate and terrible.

Hertzka, brandishing his salami-drenched copy of *Lilies of the Valley*, began a blitzkrieg of devastating proportions. Armed with the full might of International Copyright, he first attacked the luckless Lindemann in a battle that was as violent as it was brief. Lindemann handed over every copy of the song, a large amount of money, and a list of his innocent accomplices. Within a few hours the first batch had surrendered and a general rout began. Wherever the terrible Hertzka appeared, terms of submission had already been drawn up and cash—no checks were accepted, this was war—was waiting.

When it was all over, the wretched Lindemann prostrated himself in Room 618 of the Adlon Hotel. Hertzka, gracefully, consented to publish *Trink, Trink* himself, using Lindemann's spirited lyrics and cutting him in with a baby lamb's share. Everybody else had to stop forthwith, had to destroy their stocks, melt their plates, pulverize their records, and hand over the loot. The hunt was over.

For a long time the smell of the barbecue lingered in the director's room at Universal. Frobenius had been delicious and Ehrenreich's stuffed head over the mantel was lovely to look at. Copyright, sure, was wonderful.

And then I came to the United States to find things even more exciting. First I had to learn a few basic facts. In Europe, and for that matter almost everywhere else in the world, the author obtains full copyright of his work by the simple act of creation. He writes, composes, sculpts, or paints, and the law, at once, embraces his work tenderly as if it were a human life. It cannot be murdered, raped, or sold into slavery. Its very existence is enough to protect it. No forms, fees, or applications are required. Protection is given for the author's lifetime and, in most countries, for fifty years after his death.

Not so in the United States. There is no inherent birthright of a work of art. Definite steps have to be undertaken to protect it. A piece of music has to be sent to Washington, it has to be entered in the Register of Copyright, formal notice of copyright must be affixed to every copy. There are specified fees, forms, terms. If they are all complied with, down to the letter, the law will grant a maximum protection of fifty-six years. The author may outlive them if he is foolish enough to write his hit song at the age of seventeen, the heirs most certainly will—but that's all he can get. The fifty-six years are divided into two periods of twenty-eight years each. After the first twenty-eight years have elapsed, the second period has to be secured by again following definite prescribed formalities. If it isn't done at the proper time, by the proper people, in the proper form, the work fades into the public domain, and if it ever gets there, nothing can bring it back.

These are the cold facts. But again I have seen them glow magically in the golden light of life. This time it isn't hunting we go. We see, instead, the ardent swain walking towards lovers' lane, a greedy arm around an unsuspecting widow. Beware, oh widow. He is no swain. He is a publisher knowing that your husband's song is coming up for copyright renewal. Twenty-eight fateful years have gone by since he wrote it. Don't you remember? Be careful. He doesn't want your heart. He wants your signature.

I was then working for the firm of Blondie and Abner, the music publishers of Paris, Sydney, Capetown, Buenos Aires, London, Toronto, and New York. They were the publishers of a famous song, the ballad *City of Light*, which had enjoyed tremendous sales for twenty-eight years and was now coming up "for renewal." Memorandums were teletyped around the globe to make sure that no one would slip up on the job, and a junior partner even canceled a projected trip to the Moon, where he was due to open still another branch of the enterprise.

The composer of *City of Light* had long since died. It was known that he had a widow, but nobody had ever bothered with her. The composer had sold the song for fifty dollars to Blondie; no royalties had ever been paid to him or his heirs and no communication had ever been established with the widow. This, now, became a problem of serious proportions. Under the American law, her signature was necessary to obtain a copyright renewal and additional twenty-eight years of undisturbed possession and exploitation of the song.

As the deadline approached, the search grew from intense to hysterical. Newspaper ads were placed, detectives scouted the forty-eight states, rewards were posted.

With only two weeks to go, and after thousands had been spent in the search, the evasive widow was found. She was living with a new husband in a small town in South Carolina. A clerk, conspicuous more for his homespun looks than for any qualities of the mind, was dispatched to present the documents for her signature. He also carried a charming letter from Blondie and Abner and a little gift—I think it was a $2.50 bottle of perfume— to the lady. He returned three days later. He brought back the perfume and the documents. They were not signed.

He had found the widow, all right, and she was the right widow, no doubt. But she had not been alone. Her new husband had been sitting there in the living room all the time and so had a New York lawyer. The lady would be happy to sign, the husband had let it be known through the lawyer, but there ought to be some consideration. They had been thinking of a bonus of ten thousand dollars and a new contract with the usual royalty rates and a little extra. If that was agreeable, would Homespun please come back within a week—there wasn't much time to be lost and several other publishers were practically camping on their doorsill.

For several hours the midtown area of Manhattan echoed with terrible gnashing of teeth. At last common sense won the upper hand. Homespun was sent on another trip. He left the ten thousand dollars with the husband and brought back the widow's signature. The copyright renewals were dispatched to Washington and duly acknowledged. A secure period of another twenty-eight happy years dawned on the horizon.

A year passed. *City of Light* had been published in more than thirty arrangements. The copyright in every one of them had been carefully renewed: six different keys of the song, the arrangements for SA, SSA, SSTTBB, and TB, settings for flute, for harmonica, for organ, band, and piano. No loopholes had been left open, no chances taken.

But there are evil men who read the annual publications of the Register of Copyright, huge tomes of no interest to the population at large but perused by a few with the ardent devotion normal citizens apply to the Kinsey reports. They study through sleepless nights, looking for little oddities here, a forgotten bit of business there—and out of the ash can of neglected rights they lift little trinkets of gold that still wear well. It was one of these beachcombers of music who read the imposing list of copyright renewals for the *City of Light*. He read it again. Something seemed funny. Something in the proud parade of titles and figures didn't sound right.

He went back twenty-eight years. There, in the copyright register, was the same list of titles, six keys of the song, octavos, flute, heckelphone, everything properly entered and properly renewed. Still something bothered him. He took out the neighboring volume, the one *preceding* the book he had just so diligently perused, and his heart took a leap. *City of Light*, he read in the index, page 48 col. II. He opened the book. There it was. The *City of Light*, same composer, same publisher, had been entered as a song *a full year earlier* than the list of titles that had been renewed after so diligent and expensive a hunt.

He kept on digging. What he found sounded almost incredible. *City of Light* had indeed been published by Abner and Blondie once before and properly entered for copyright. Then some mistakes had been discovered—the edition had been withdrawn. The new print, made the following year, had started the tidal wave of success. Nobody ever remembered the earlier *fausse couche*. Nobody but the man who looked through the ash can.

Twenty-nine, not twenty-eight, fateful years had elapsed since *City of Light* had first been published! One year too many had gone down the river of time and nobody could ever bring it back. The *City of Light* was in the public domain.

A terrible cry went out from Blondie and Abner. It soon shrank into a miserable whimper. There was nothing anybody could do.

The victory of the diligent reader of copyright registers was as short-lived as it had been brilliant. Dozens of other publishers soon started printing the song. Recording companies stopped payments, ASCAP struck the corpse from the list of the living, the price of a sheet copy, fifty wonderful cents for twenty-eight wonderful years, dropped to a nickel.

Only the widow rejoiced. She had the ten thousand dollars, and she needed money, too. She had decided to send her boy to college to become a copyright lawyer.

Trying and difficult as all this is, even in so simple a matter as the dealings with a widow in South Carolina, it becomes a fascinating abyss of confusion as we enter the denser regions, the deeply entangled forest of international copyright.

Up to 1891, when the first American Copyright Act was passed, no foreign composer or author could obtain copyright in this country (unless he was a resident of the United States). He enjoyed protection under the common law as long as his work remained manuscript. Publication at once took it forever out of his hands.

What this meant in practical life is strikingly illustrated by the legal adventures of Gilbert and Sullivan in America. *H.M.S. Pinafore* had been their first great hit in this country. In 1879 an announcement in a newspaper stated that "at present there are forty-two companies playing *Pinafore* about the country. Companies formed after 6 P.M. are not included." Fortunes were made, but not a single dime went to the authors. The work had been published in England. It had no protection whatsoever in the United States.

Gilbert and Sullivan, obviously, didn't like it. "We determined," says Sullivan in his book of memoirs, "to produce our next opera in the States first and in Great Britain afterwards. The Americans acknowledge that the author has a right in his *unpublished* work in the same way that he could lay claim to his own personal apparel or any other form of property, and only lost his prerogative after it had been published. So all we could do was to follow this course, to produce our piece in America and to get our own company well under way before others could print their imitations."

On December 31, 1879, they produced the *Pirates of Penzance* at the Fifth Avenue Theatre in New York—and a merry New Year's Eve it must have been. "Of course," Sir Arthur reports, "at that time there was no copyright between the two countries, and so we were compelled to retain possession of the whole work in manuscript. To have stolen that from us would have made the thief not less amenable under the common law than anyone who, for example, might try to get hold of one's purse. But if we had published it and had proceeded against the thief who had made use of the opera, we should have had to take action against him under the statute law and should have failed."

Even such cautious procedure, however, provided no real security. "As some judges felt that theatrical representation was tantamount to publication," Sir Arthur continues, "any member of the audience who managed to take down the libretto in shorthand and succeeded in memorizing the music was quite at liberty to produce his own version of the work. This made matters exciting: we kept a sharp lookout, and if anyone in the theater was observed taking notes or anything of the kind, the note-taker was promptly turned out."

Members of the orchestra had to be kept under constant surveillance: they were offered bribes if they would take their orchestral parts—particularly the coveted first violin, which contained a particello of the score—out of the theater after a performance, leaving it at some pre-arranged spot where a crew of copyists was waiting. It was, as Sullivan says, "a constant state of guerilla warfare."

These and similar incidents finally became an international outrage. The American position had to be adjusted after, in 1886, all European countries (with the exception of Russia) bounded together in a pact, the Bern Convention, for the mutual protection of their citizens.

The United States never joined. The Bern Convention, presented to the Senate by President Cleveland, was rejected—its provisions could never be reconciled with the basically different conceptions of American legal thinking. But five years later Congress accepted the principle of international copyright. Works of foreigners can now enjoy the full protection of the American law. A presidential proclamation, recognizing that a condition of reciprocity exists, has to be issued for each individual country.

The first proclamations admitted Belgians, Frenchmen, Britishers, Swiss, Germans, and Italians. But many important music-producing countries were admitted only many years later—Austria, for instance, in 1907, and Hungary, native country of Franz Lehár and many of his successful colleagues, as late as 1912 (*The Merry Widow* has never enjoyed copyright in America). All this had devastating consequences for authors and composers, and created a state of deep, never-ending confusion among music users in the United States.

Verdi's operas were never protected in the United States, with the sole exception of *Falstaff*, published in 1893, one year after the United States and Italy had established copyright relations. That was too late, however, both for Mascagni and Leoncavallo, whose celebrated twin-bill never netted them a cent in America. When in 1918, at the close of World War I, a whole crop of new countries sprang into existence—Finland, Poland, Czechoslovakia, Yugoslavia, among others—none of them had, of course, a copyright agreement with the United States. In the troublesome postwar years weightier matter had to be tackled first. Only in 1927 and 1928 were most of them admitted by presidential proclamation. The music written during the vacuum remains unprotected. The man who probably suffered most from this situation is Jan Sibelius, who gets eighty-two boxes of cigars as a birthday present from a grateful America but no royalties for in-

numerable performances of many of his most successful
works.

A very special niche, or rather dunce corner, is reserved
to Russian composers. Russia has never established copyright relations with the United States. No Russian citizen
can obtain protection. Czar or Stalin, the imperial Rach-
maninoff or the marxian Shostakovitch, Rimsky-Korsakov
or Khatchaturian, it's all the same. Igor Stravinsky had
the bad luck to write his most celebrated pieces—*Pulci-
nella, Petrouchka, Sacre du Printemps,* and similar high-
lights of his life—while he still retained Russian citizenship. They obtained full protection in Europe and all the
countries of the Bern Convention because Koussevitzky
published them first in his *Editions Russe de Musique* in
Berlin and Paris. This had been an established custom in
Europe. Every Russian publisher—Belaieff, Bessel, even
the new Soviet State Publishing House—had branches
in Leipzig, Berlin, or Paris and made sure to release their
publications there at least one day before they were to
announce them in Moscow. A whole generation of Russian composers thus obtained the full protection of the
Bern Convention countries where protection depends on
the place of publication. The citizenship of the composer
does not enter the picture.

Not so in the United States. From Tchaikovsky to
Prokofieff no Russian has been granted copyright. Stravinsky, now an American citizen, has been rewriting some
of his scores and, as an American, has obtained copyright
protection for the "new version" of *Petrouchka* and other

works. The famous originals cannot be affected. They are lost to him forever.

Others—and these are the saddest and most confusing cases—just didn't pay any attention to American regulations. Ravel, for example, instructed his publishers not to waste money by sending the required entry fee—one dollar!—to Washington: America, then, meant nothing to him and many other European composers and publishers. His *Jeux d'Eau*, his famous *Pavane*, his *Alborada del Gracioso* were deliberately never registered in Washington and have always been in the public domain. So were some of Richard Strauss's tone poems. I have often wondered what Strauss said—he who liked money perhaps more than any composer I have met, and I have seen greedy birds in my time—when he found out, too late, that his publishers, Joseph Aibl of Munich, had saved three dollars and a copy of the scores and thus thrown, forever, into the public domain in America such priceless royalty producers as *Don Juan*, *Death and Transfiguration*, and *Till Eulenspiegel*.

Here are a few of the most celebrated pieces that are outstanding examples of this strange twist of fate. They are protected for fifty years after the death of the author in the rest of the civilized world but have never been protected in the United States:

Bartók (d. in 1945)	All his earlier works, including the famous *Children's Pieces*—everything written before Hungary and the

United States established copyright relations in 1912.

DEBUSSY (1918)

Afternoon of a Faun. (Careful now: The Childfiend-DeBussy arrangement enjoys full copyright protection in this country and must not be tampered with for fifty-six years. You can rape Debussy but you mustn't rape Childfiend.)

DUKAS (1935)

The Sorcerer's Apprentice.

DVOŘÁK (1904)

New World Symphony. The fate of this work is particularly odd. Not only is it dedicated to the New World; it was actually written while the composer lived in the United States and performed, for the first time, in his presence, in Carnegie Hall in New York in 1893. But Dvořák was not a legal resident of the country where and to whose greater glory the symphony was written and, as the United States did not establish copyright relations with his native Austria till 1907, the New World never granted protection (or paid any royalties to the composer) for the symphony that bears its name!

ELGAR (1934)	*Enigma Variations.* (Lapsed into public domain due to a slip-up by the publisher who did not claim the renewal rights in time.)
FAURÉ (1924)	All of his most celebrated songs.
GRIEG (1907)	Practically all of Grieg's music has never been copyrighted in the United States.
HUMPERDINCK (1921)	*Hansel and Gretel.*
LEHÁR (1948)	*The Merry Widow. Gold and Silver Waltz.*
LEONCAVALLO (1919)	*Pagliacci.*
MASCAGNI (1945)	*Cavalleria Rusticana.*
MASSENET (1912)	*Manon.*
RAVEL (1937)	*Pavane pour une Infante Défunte, Alborada del Gracioso.*
SAINT-SAËNS (1921)	*Samson and Dalila.*
SIBELIUS	*Finlandia, Swan of Tuonela, Second Symphony.*
STRAUSS (1951)	*Don Juan, Death and Transfiguration, Till Eulenspiegel.*
STRAVINSKY	*Petrouchka, Pulcinella, Sacre du Printemps.*

Wonderful music—and all for free.

CORTÈGE

How fast the day goes. So late already and so much still to do, so much to remember, so much music still to be heard.

I have to close my eyes for a while. It's quiet now out in the courtyard, in the heat of noon. Major and Minor sit motionless, sleepily burying their heads in the puffy cloud of their feathers. The girl in the office across is gone—maybe the lover she had been pleading with so ardently has come back, or the mortgage has been extended, or the doctor has come to see the old mother at last—somewhere, out there in the tremendous town.

Let me close the door and shut off the phone for a few minutes. The music outside can wait. There are other voices to be listened to—the voices of the silent pictures at my wall, ever present, smiling, safe.

The music outside, the hum of the city,

the shouts and the haste are stilled as the silent voices become stronger and the faded eyes begin to glow again with life, laughter, and love.

I had met Béla Bartók many years ago in Europe when I was a young man with Universal Edition in Vienna, his publishers. Frequently he came through Vienna on his way to or from his native Budapest, and every time his short, businesslike calls were very special occurrences in the routine of our establishment. He was already an important composer, famous in an esoteric, not easily defined way, but not at all successful if success is measured by the usual yardstick of earth-bound public acclaim. Yet his visits—never improvised, always announced in a formal letter which stated not only the day but the exact hour of his appearance, arrangements which he would keep unfailingly—caused nervous fear and uneasiness. The deep respect extended to him by everybody from the doorman to the president of Universal was of a special brand, an intensity and seriousness that was rarely rendered any other of the many famous composers who walked through our doors from morning to night. Even the great Arnold Schönberg, so terrible in his wrath and so easily hurt by a wrong word or a seeming lack of submission, could sometimes quite easily be pacified by a well-placed joke or induced to tell a couple of them himself, and if he could get in a pun he came right down from his pedestal, grinning and relaxed, enjoying himself tremendously and becoming almost human. Bartók lived in

an unsmiling, hushed world where there was little room
for our human frailties and no pardon for our sins.

When he arrived in America in the winter of 1940, on
what was to be his last and final trip, our connection
became much closer. I worked at that time for the music
publishing house of Boosey & Hawkes, who in the meantime had become Bartók's publishers. Some of his most
celebrated works were written and prepared for publication during that period, among them the famous *Concerto for Orchestra*. The intense and often complicated
administration of his musical output kept us in almost
daily communication, even during the summer months
when I used to call on him regularly at a primitive little
summerhouse in Saranac Lake.

The contacts were intensified by the fact that Boosey &
Hawkes, in order to assist Bartók and his wife, the pianist
Dita Pasztory, in their attempts to get engagements on
the concert stage, had started a little concert bureau of
their own. Thus I worked for him in a double capacity,
as publisher and as manager, to the last day of his life.

In his own time, and even more today, after the radiation of his work has grown beyond anything he himself
had ever experienced, Béla Bartók has been referred to as
"the great Hungarian composer." He was Hungarian, of
course, in the technical sense of the word, and he loved
his country. His music had its roots deep in his native
soil. Before he died he was visibly moved by his nomina-
tion to the new Hungarian Parliament, shortly after the
country had been liberated from German occupation.

Yet one could never think of him as a Hungarian, or, for that matter, as belonging to any nation, group, or race. He was a human being, pure, strict, of an almost abstract, sidereal quality, governed only by the laws of decency, integrity, and faith, which he applied uncompromisingly to his own conduct and whose breach by others he never forgave.

His angelic righteousness made him unfit for a world where everything has become a give-and-take, where every hand washed every other hand, and where there was an angle to everything. He neither knew of nor tolerated angles. In his music as well as in his life the very thought that he would ever compromise, accommodate himself to the demands of the day, to practical considerations, to any detour from what he felt to be right, was unthinkable. He would never take the easy way, always the hard one.

How it all comes back to me now as I look at the picture here, at the wall. The penetrating, clear, oh so serious eyes staring at me again, demanding, quiet, uncompromising. The beautiful, wise face: calm, stern, seldom ruffled by a short, rapidly subsiding wave of bitter, puckish laughter.

He was shy, very quiet-spoken, constantly on the alert, suspicious of everyone and everything. Never did I hear him raise his voice. When others would shout he would clam up, retire silently, his face even more drawn, into an icy sphere of disapproval that was much more difficult to take and to dispel again than any temperamental out-

burst would have been. He was small, almost tiny, terribly frail. His thin body, the sharply pointed nose, the
noble forehead with the soft, silken hair, the transparent,
childlike hands, the slow, swinging walk (as if he walked
on clouds)—his was the appearance of an ascetic, a
thinker, a brooder, a ponderer, never at ease, relentlessly
driven by an inner flame that eventually consumed him
in the very sense of the word.

The first impression that struck me when I saw him
again here in America was how little he had changed. His
hair had become white, but his face, his eyes, his body
seemed never to change in all the years I knew him. He
seemed quite ageless—he had never looked really young,
and even through the years of his sickness he changed
little outwardly.

He had come to America as a refugee under the most
trying, difficult, and forbidding circumstances. Again, in
taking upon himself a fate that he shared with thousands,
he was quite alone. If ever anyone chose freedom for no
other reason than because he could not live without it, it
was Béla Bartók.

Neither he nor his wife was Jewish, and no racial uneasiness prompted him to choose emigration as a way to
safety. Nor did any political associations make it advis-
able to leave. A single *Heil!* would have been sufficient to
make him safe and comfortable. He had a secure income as a professor at the Royal Conservatory of Music
in Budapest, a house, a pension for his latter days, his
books, his garden, his vast collection of folk music from

many countries—Hungary, Rumania, North Africa, Tur-
key—which he had noted down and recorded in decades
of scientific work. He had his own language, his lifelong
friends, the beloved surroundings of home. Nothing compelled him to leave it all and to seek the precarious shel-
ter of a foreign shore: nothing but his unbending heart,
his complete and absolute inability to compromise, to
make peace—even with lip service—with the forces of
evil. Compromise was unthinkable. It would have destroyed his very soul.

In leaving, he risked much more than many a famous
man would have risked who stayed on, took the devil's
blood money, and counted—quite correctly—on the for-
getfulness and forgiveness of the world. Bartók's was not
a glamorous name, sure to be accepted by the western
world and to be safely installed in a new existence of
honor and wealth. When he set out with his wife and his
son on the perilous journey—weeks of traveling through
Europe, their baggage lost somewhere in Spain, barely
reaching Lisbon for the freighter that brought them across
—he faced an uncertain future: poverty, a violent climate,
disruption of his scientific work, a city whose noises and
nervous vibrations pounded day and night at his emaci-
ated body and supersensitive mind. He also was to face an
artistic hierarchy, too busy with the advancement of their
own glory to pay much attention to the quiet, small man
who could be hurt with one unguarded word and repudi-
ated forever with the shrug of a shoulder.

But there was never, in the years of his exile, either

doubt or regret. His determination, as always, was absolute. After he had put the ocean between himself and the enemies of everything he had been living for, he even refused to speak or to write German. He spoke, instead, a very selected, highly cultivated English, slightly stilted, choosing his words slowly, striving perceptibly always to find the right expression. His speech retained a quite undefinable foreign flavor. It was highly civilized, rich, and often amazing in its variety of vocabulary and the elegance of its grammar. Even when we were alone and when the conversation might have been easier and much less of a strain on both of us if conducted in German, he would never use the language of the enemy.

His letters, too, ever since he had come to America, were always written in English, composed by the hand of a master and just as dense in their texture as they had been in the old days. Only once in a while he would question with a (?) his own proper use of a word or a phrase, sensing infallibly the slightest error or foreignism in a language he had spoken for only a short time.

Bartók's letters were always written by hand, in a small, clear script that looked as if every word had been put down slowly and deliberately. Every thought, it seemed, had been completed in his mind before it was put on paper, just as if the words were musical notes, the result of an intense process of formulation. There were no unnecessary phrases in these letters and, wherever possible, he used postcards, filling them to the edge. Neither time nor space was ever wasted on courtesies, on how-do-you-dos, on anything personal that had no connection with the subject of his message. When, after his death, we went through his letters to help provide "human interest" material for a man who wanted to write Bartók's biography, we found almost nothing that would shed light on his character or his life.

The letters covered the paper from top to bottom. Even the margin was usually used for a postscript or two. If the letter did not fill the page, he would tear off what wasn't used, mailing only a closely covered scrap of paper. His room was always overflowing with little paper strips and torn-off pieces of printed matter, every one of them covered with notes, figures, symbols, and a special musical shorthand understandable only to him. All these notes, clippings, letters, books, manuscript paper, music, were scattered throughout the room, overflowing from the piano to the floor, covering chairs and tables—an appalling accumulation. Seemingly aimlessly scattered throughout the room, they were in reality exciting witness to a mind that never rested and was occupied, simultaneously, with many problems and ideas. Every one of them was always present and ready to be consulted whenever he would have need of them.

New York was the powerful, unconquerable enemy. Traffic frightened him deeply. He would never walk against a light, and even when he crossed with a green light he was tense and disturbed, hurrying across the street in short, hasty steps, like an animal that has left his protecting woods, and faces, wide-eyed, the roaring uncertainties of the metropolis. The climate, New York heat and New York cold alike, was a constant source of preoccupation. Noise, and particularly any emanation of music penetrating his privacy, caused him physical suffering. The vicinity of a radio meant painful disruption of his creative work.

Sometimes he seemed to delight, in a strange and almost self-destructive way, in the difficulties and setbacks he experienced; he used to relate them in great detail, an ironical "I told you so" in his voice. At the same time, he would discard any good news we had for him with a deep-rooted disbelief that his fortunes would ever take a decisive and permanent turn for the better. The difficulties of finding an apartment where he and his wife would be allowed to practice were at first insurmountable. When, finally, friends located a place in Forest Hills where practicing pianists were not regarded as breachers of the peace, he only shrugged his shoulders—there would be other difficulties, he asserted. And he was right. After the Bartóks had moved in and the two pianos had been delivered by an obliging manufacturer, it was discovered that they could not be placed in one room. Triumphantly Bartók reported that they had to practice in two different rooms, separated by a corridor, unable to see each other, with coordination established only by ear.

During the first year or two after his arrival, Bartók appeared as soloist with a few symphony orchestras, but dates were few and scattered. The joint recitals he gave with his wife were not too successful. The programs he chose reflected, again, his uncompromising mind. Not too many organizations were prepared to forgo the commercial appeal of other two-piano teams for the unbending austerity of the Bartóks. The fact that they never performed from memory proved an added handicap. Their appearance on the stage in the company of two page-turners seemed old-fashioned and was easily misinterpreted as a lack of preparation or courtesy by audiences that had been treated to flashier displays of virtuosity.

And Béla Bartók's bows were certainly a concert manager's nightmare; stern, professorial, unsmiling to the extent of chilliness—of a great, very moving dignity, but bare of everything the public had been trained to expect from a performer. Nothing, of course, that anyone would ever dare to suggest to him would change his attitude toward his programs and their presentation, and his hopes to earn a livelihood on the concert stage were sadly disappointed. Later, as his illness progressed, even the few concert appearances and lecture recitals we had been able to book for him had to be canceled.

Life was grim. Offers to accept a position as a teacher of composition—they had come from several educational institutions—he turned down unwaveringly. He was determined not to teach composition, the one thing everybody wanted him to teach. He seemed to feel he had nothing to teach, nothing to give to others in the one field where he was great, an undisputed master! He was willing to teach piano, but only a few private pupils stud-

ied with him for short periods. He accepted, though, a
few scientific assignments. One of them, offered by Columbia University, kept him busy for two years and provided him with a slim, academic salary.

He had, during that time, a little studio in one of the
brownstone houses owned by the university on 117th
Street. Here he spent several hours each day, transcribing
on paper a great number of recordings which had been
made in various European countries: folk songs, dances,
and melodies, played and sung by the shepherds and peas-
ants of eastern and southeastern Europe, all very difficult
in rhythm and intonation, decipherable only by a highly
trained and incredibly patient mind and a sensitive ear.
These notations, a unique mixture of scholarly exactness
and creative genius, were just as close to his heart as his
own music. With infinite, tireless care he listened to thousands of recordings, wrote down the tunes in all their in-
flections and variations, using his own method of musical
notation to put them faithfully on paper. Detailed foot-
notes and carefully worded explanations, minute in every
detail, accompanied most of them.

And this was the same spirit that dreamed up the
powerful pages of his own music, freely soaring through
fantastic space, trying the impossible, speaking with Pro-
metheus' fiery tongues—only to return again to the pains-
takingly accurate realm of science.

The Columbia assignment, limited as it was in scope,
had been a great help. It had provided the composer with

a minimum of security; and regularity of income was, to Bartók's methodical mind, the only possible way to make a livelihood. Many of the composers it has been my good fortune to be associated with conducted their lives under the assumption that everybody—publishers, agents, opera directors, symphony orchestras, juke boxes, and heirs—would make mountains of money from their works as soon as they died. They decided—not, it appears, without some justification—that they might as well cash in on all this while they themselves were still around. They saw no reason to balance their books. They felt fully justified in borrowing on posthumous glory.

To Bartók such imaginary bookkeeping was unthinkable. When we had, at last, persuaded him to accept an advance on his royalties, he insisted that the full amount be deducted at the end of the year. His young son had joined the American Navy soon after the family's arrival in this country. He was glad to know that his pay was regularly sent to the father; the boy didn't need it and was happy to help. But when he came home the father handed him a bankbook. There he found every penny he had been paid throughout the war years. "It wasn't mine," the father told him. "It's yours." Béla Bartók's views about money were never those of an artist. They were those of a puritan, and they were sometimes quite exasperating.

During a previous visit to the United States he had made a few recordings of his piano works for one of the smaller companies in New York. The owner of the business, an American of Hungarian descent, was a great admirer of Bartók. He called me one day; he wanted to come up and see me. It was rather important, he said.

What he proposed was startling. He knew that it was quite impossible to offer Bartók any money he didn't think he had earned. So he had devised a scheme whereby he would forge the royalty statements he was about to send to the composer. Instead of accounting for the few hundred records he had actually sold, he would show a sale of 10,897. Royalties would be paid for that amount. The statement, as was usual, was to be sent to the composer through us, his publishers: even the slightest deviation would have aroused Bartók's suspicion. Our book-keeper became part of the plot, entries were made to substantiate the crime, and statement and check went out to the composer.

When I saw Bartók a few days later, he asked me at once whether I had seen the statement. He was very pleased, happily excited. I felt miserable. Even if this was a conspiracy I could always be proud of, such a deceit seemed almost criminal in his presence.

A few days later he called me on the phone. "I want you to take steps against Columbia Records," he said. In a sudden foreboding of what had happened, I felt my swivel chair turn into molasses.

He explained that he had just received another statement for gramophone records sold, this one from Columbia. They accounted for 349 copies.

"It's quite impossible," Bartók said, quietly but in stern determination. "Here is a little company selling 10,897 records, and at the same time a big outfit like Columbia sells a few hundred. I want you to investigate."

Somehow, with the help of the man who had pushed me into this web of benevolent deceit, I got out of it; but it took a lot of very nervous explaining, and once in a while I was sure that Bartók suspected me of being in conspiracy not with the real culprit but with the innocent accounting department of Columbia. At last the incident was pushed aside—I wouldn't say forgotten, since Bartók never forgot anything—as a more important event took the stage: the strange circumstances surrounding the creation of Bartók's last big work, the *Concerto for Orchestra*.

In the spring of 1943 the sickness that had gripped him for some time had worsened noticeably. He was running a temperature, regularly, at certain hours of the day. He followed the symptoms with visible apprehension. He became weaker, more irritable, more difficult to approach. He had to cancel lectures and instructed us not to book him for recitals any more—he was sure he would be unable to appear in public again. He turned down a scientific assignment offered him, in spite of the fact that the university which made the offer explained that he was welcome to the honorarium and could begin work at any time, no matter how indefinite, in the future. But so deeply was he filled with his sense of responsibility that he was unwilling to accept as long as he was not absolutely sure that he would be able to deliver his part of the bargain. Sometimes it was very difficult to have to deal with so stubborn a display of angelic principles.

At last he could not stay any longer in the dingy apartment on Fifty-seventh Street and Eighth Avenue where he had been living lately. He was brought to a hospital at the East River. For some time ASCAP, the American Society of Composers, Authors and Publishers, had provided him, at their expense, with the best medical specialists. To their eternal honor—Bartók was not even, in a technical sense, a member, belonging to the British Performing Right Society in London—they now made themselves responsible for the costs of the hospital as well.

Serious as his physical condition already was, it seemed to be aggravated by the growing feeling of solitude and bitterness that had taken hold of him. He saw himself as a neglected stranger, away from the main flow of musical activity in America. Once in a while he remembered with bitter nostalgia the days of his European past. The artists and conductors who played his music in America were, to a large extent, old acquaintances, many of them former Hungarians. Only a few of the great stars showed interest in his music, and when Yehudi Menuhin played his *Violin Concerto*, Bartók was so deeply moved by the unexpected attention of a great artist that he wrote a new sonata for Menuhin.

But now all this was forgotten as the composer was brooding, sick, poor, in the enforced inactivity of a hospital room. We had little to cheer him up. Small things didn't matter. There were no big ones to report.

It was then, in the summer of 1943, that something happened in the room in Doctors Hospital in New York that strangely and mysteriously resembles an event in another sickroom 152 years earlier: the sudden appearance of the "mysterious stranger," who had come to commission the dying Mozart to write the *Requiem*. This time, in streamlined New York, the messenger was no mystery man. He was a well-clad, elegant gentleman of very aristocratic bearing. His name was Serge Koussevitzky.

The visit came as an unexpected surprise to the sick composer. Koussevitzky was one of the conductors who had never played any of Bartók's important scores. I don't think that the two men had ever met before. Koussevitzky most certainly was the last man Bartók, bitter, sick, thinking himself rejected by the public and the leading men of music in America, could ever imagine crossing his door.

The conductor was alone. He took a chair, moved it close to the bed, and began to explain his mission. He had come to offer Béla Bartók a commission from the Koussevitzky Foundation—a commission carrying one thousand dollars—and the assurance of a first performance by the Boston Symphony Orchestra. The composer was free to choose any form of music he cared to write. There was just one condition: the score was to be dedicated to the memory of Mrs. Natalie Koussevitzky, the conductor's wife, who had died a few years earlier and in whose memory the foundation had been established. It was to be a Requiem, after all!

Koussevitzky himself later told me the details of the conversation, and as he recalled it he seemed genuinely moved. Bartók, touched without doubt by the personal appearance of the conductor, who could have sent a letter or had the message delivered by one of his countless disciples, declined. He could not accept money for a work he might never be able to write.

The conductor had been prepared for just this situation. Before the foundation had decided to give the commission to Bartók, friends of the composer (Fritz Reiner and Joseph Szigeti among others) had approached Koussevitzky and the members of his board of trustees, urging that Bartók be choosen. They had impressed on them his precarious circumstances and the difficulty of helping the proud man with anything he might consider charity. It had to be a real commission, even if, due to Bartók's delicate health, nothing whatever came of it.

Koussevitzky explained to the reluctant composer that he was bound by the trustees' decision. A commission, once decided upon, could not be taken back. The money was given to him no matter whether he was willing or able to deliver the piece. These were the terms of the covenant. He had, in fact, under the rules of the foundation, already brought with him a check for five hundred dollars—which he was obliged to leave with Bartók, together with an official letter stating the terms of the commission.

Bartók made no reply. He suddenly began talking of other matters. He asked the conductor, almost urgently, to stay on. The two men had a long talk. Bartók did most of the talking, unburdening his troubled mind. He covered many subjects and became flushed with a new and very touching confidence in life. It was almost an hour later that the nurse came in and the conductor took his leave.

Undoubtedly the learned specialists who attended Béla Bartók in the sickness which two years later consumed what was left of him will have more logical explanations for the incredible recovery that set in almost immediately after Koussevitzky's visit. All we know is that soon they found him to be so much better that they released him from the hospital. He left New York for Asheville, North Carolina. He found a quiet room in the outskirts where neither traffic lights nor radios interfered with the absolute concentration that he craved. At last he smelled fresh air again, saw the sky, felt the soil. The Hearst Building, the Fiske Building, the entrance to the Independent Subway station, the newsstand, the assortment of sweat and dirt he had viewed from his window on Fifty-seventh Street were replaced by flowers and trees. And the constantly tormenting screams of auto horns and police sirens were drowned in memory by the concert of birds. Their cries and calls can be heard in the second movement of Bartók's *Third Piano Concerto*, which he sketched in Asheville and completed, with the exception of seventeen bars, in a grim race with death in the summer of 1945. He had returned to the sources of nature. In the last pages he ever wrote, the Hungarian, the European, the great citizen of the world set a small, lovely monument to the birds of North Carolina. . . .

He was happy again. "Don't send me special-delivery letters or telegrams," he wrote us a few days after he had arrived in Asheville. "I get all my mail only once a day. Everything is delivered at the same time—mail, papers, special deliveries, wires. Here, time makes no difference." He had no piano. Once in a while his room was very cold. He went for walks, always alone. There was nobody to talk to, only one family where he occasionally took a meal and where he would practice the piano from time to time. He asked us to send them a selection of his music as a token of his gratitude.

His letters, deviating strangely from the austerity we had come to expect, sounded almost elated. He included short health bulletins, giving us a graph of his morning and night temperatures with slightly ironic but not at all pessimistic comments. Most important of all, he asked for music paper—lots of it. Then, suddenly, he wrote that he had completed a major part of a new work he was writing for Serge Koussevitzky. He was sending us the score to be copied. Soon a second and a final third batch arrived. It was the *Concerto for Orchestra*.

He did not return from Asheville in time to be present at its tumultuous première in Boston in December 1944. But he observed its immediate success, its acceptance as one of the great masterpieces of our generation. He knew that this time he had touched the hearts of his audiences, and he was present to hear it and take many of his gentle, very touching, terribly serious bows when the work was played in New York.

When I saw him a few months later, he rested, at last. The little funeral parlor on Lexington Avenue in Manhattan was filled with a hushed, deeply stirred crowd. There were no representatives of organizations, no honorary pallbearers, nobody who had come because he wanted to be sure that his name would be in the register. I don't believe that there was a register. No reporters were there, no pictures were taken as the mourners, stunned, filed out.

But there were many people who had not known him and who had suddenly felt that they must come to pay their respects. Suddenly, this very day, he had become great. As I took a last look before they closed the coffin, I felt again, stronger than ever before, that this tiny face, so beautiful, so great in the peace of death, drawn even now by suffering and still reflecting an unending struggle, was not only the unforgettable face of a great musician. It was the face of a great man, a shining example of bravery, faith, and an indomitable spirit that will live on long after the frame that carried them has been taken back, forever, by the dust.

PHILADELPHIA
TEA PARTY

How strange the twists of fate, how close heaven to hell. If it hadn't been for my acquaintance with Béla Bartók, the most saintly man I ever met, I would probably never have known what I know today about a business that has been called every name under the sun but which even its most determined press agents would never dare to call saintly, or anything faintly associated with the regions above—the concert business in America.

What a business it is, what sweeping operation, what fantastic scheme. The ideas behind it, the force, the organization, the wealth! The frustration in its wake, the tears, the failures, the black, final despair. Of all the odd and fascinating adventures which color the tremendous scene of American musical life, this is the oddest, the biggest, the most fascinating, the most crushingly powerful, the most incredible, the most American adventure. There is nothing in the world like it.

It's a business for very big people. It isn't meant for outsiders. People who think they might help themselves to an occasional nibble are allowed to hustle around the big cheese for a little while. Then the trap snaps and the nosy intruder is carried outside. If he is lucky he can go back to a nice comfortable desk, grateful to be returned to his own world, and talk about his experiences in the artists' business to a couple of pigeons.

Soon after the Bartóks had come to New York, and while we were still in the midst of harassing conversations on how to organize their uprooted lives, another arrival from Hungary knocked at our door. He was a charming, most pleasant fellow, always smiling, full of life, and radiating a confidence in the ultimate success of anything he undertook which overwhelmed even the stoutest skeptic. His name was Hunyadi Kecscemet.

Before he had decided to switch from the banks of the Danube to the safer shores of the Hudson, or, rather, from the shores of the Danube to the safer banks of New York, he had been a concert manager in Budapest, and when you listened to him and looked at his face, beaming with happiness and supreme assurance, there couldn't have been a more successful one in all Hungary. He had always been a great and sincere admirer of Béla Bartók, he professed. We were the publishers of the great composer. What could be more logical, simple, and of greater service to everybody concerned than for us, at the same time, to manage Bartók, the pianist? Of course, in order to manage, we needed a manager. Fate, indeed, had brought us together.

That was the beginning of our Artists Bureau. Stationery was printed, a secretary hired, offices rented where any self-respecting artists bureau would rent offices: on Fifty-seventh Street, right in the midst of things. Carnegie Hall was within easy distance, Steinway Hall almost next door. A Beefburger where one could get a 6o-cent lunch was down the hall, and the Russian Tea Room, the fabulous place *Where Music, Art, and Ballet Lovers Meet*, right across the street. At the Beefburger we munched our luncheons, at the Russian Tea Room we spent our afternoons, watching an endless parade of musicians lining up for admission, scrutinized with an unbribable eye by a huge man in a blue suit who tried, desperately but with little success, to preserve the sorry remains of what once had been a fine Russian accent.

A few of them, chosen at random, were admitted, escorted grimly and with tremendous strides (which they could keep up with only by breaking into a pathetic canter) to tiny tables where they were pushed violently against the wall and turned over to a bloused waiter, a Natasha, Fjederowna Nikolajewna, or Igor, fine Americans who never heard the Volga flow. The man in the blue suit at once turned around contemptuously and returned to his post. Brandishing a huge, sharp-edged menu, he looked with deep hostility over clusters of guests who glanced at him from far below in sheepish anxiety as if, indeed, they themselves expected soon to be served as a lamb stew à la General Brusilov. Unless he liked them, they knew that they would never be admitted to the fraternity of musical borsht eaters, condemned, instead, to wilt miserably in a waiting line that never got shorter and to watch helplessly while luckier patrons passed them, chatting away gaily, laughing repulsively, rejoicing in the heart-warming knowledge that the man in the blue suit had winked at them, gratefully galloping after him to be pushed against the wall and filled with inziki, tschatanisch, and wlk.

The eating musicians seemed a carefree, happy lot. Only rarely did I see the flame of hate, usually carefully buried under a greasy layer of smiles, suddenly break out, singeing a delicious *boeuf Stroganoff*; and the viper of jealousy, hidden in lovely, very visible bosoms, was almost never allowed to show its glittering head and to drop a generous portion of venom on the French pastry, a specialty of the house.

Hunyadi, of course, was always admitted and was at once at home there, just as he had been at home at Kempinski's in Berlin, at the Café Museum in Vienna, or at the beloved hangouts at the Octogon in Budapest. He had started operations of our Artists Bureau with immediate vehemence. In addition to Béla Bartók, one or two other composers from our own catalogue were eager to add an occasional appearance as pianist, conductor, or lecturer to their meager incomes and signed cheerfully with our cheerful manager. Within a few months additional hopefuls had succumbed to his charm—several composers, a few pianists, a fiddler or two, a viola player, a harpsichordist, and even a chamber orchestra, conducted by a gentleman married to a lady of not inconsiderable means.

It was wonderful to watch Hunyadi—or Howard, as he now called himself—at work. He had office hours from dawn to midnight and far beyond. He met trains and planes, sent flowers, mailed valentines, remembered birthdays, kissed every hand within reach. His patience was limitless, his time available to all and sundry. He escorted artists from their homes to the concert hall, sending them off to the stage with a handshake and a deep, halting look that would have instilled a rabbit with the unshakable confidence to walk out there and let go with the *E-Flat Mazurka*. He was waiting for them at intermission time, with orange juice, a dry shirt, and exuberant words of praise and comfort. He took them back to their houses, sitting up all night, making coffee, holding hands till the morning edition of the New York *Times* would bring redemption or a death sentence. If it was redemption, he would stay for breakfast; if it was death, he went home, drawing up plans for an appeal: the next recital that was sure to bring not only a commutation of the sentence but full vindication, victory, and fame.

He arranged auditions with conductors, women's committees, and local managers from Corpus Christi, radiating confidence when there was every reason to radiate despair. When an infant was born to one of his artists or an uncle passed away in Ecuador, there was no joy and no grief that would equal his.

How I admired him! He was everything a concertizing artist could ask for: a manager of infinite patience, tact, knowledge, and imagination; a private secretary, a psychoanalyst, a nurse, a porter, a haberdasher, a baby sitter, a throat specialist, a father-confessor, a banker, a valet, a travel agent, an alarm clock, a shoulder to weep on, an echo, and a door mat. And he had nerves of steel.

I realized the full measure of his towering strength only when I was called upon, from time to time, to take his place while he was roaming the land in one of his booking trips, excursions into the wide-open spaces which he loved so much even if he couldn't pronounce them. It was particularly one of these, thank heaven rare and in-between occasions, that made me understand that managers are born, not made, and that pinch hitters can never take the place of the real hero of the game.

Howard, by an incredible stroke of luck and genius, had prevailed on no less a personage than Sir Thomas Beecham, Bart., to trust his American fortunes to our little outfit. Sir Thomas was the brightest if not the only feather in our cap, giving the undertaking impetus, glamour, and sorely needed cash.

Sir Thomas's appearances as a guest with leading American orchestras, flamboyant and artistically brilliant as they were, had not always the desired result in the stony field of public relations. His luncheon speeches, interviews, impromptu addresses from the podium, and similar extramusical activities more often than not undid most of the good his enchanting baton had done. Several important orchestras had taken offense. Bookings became more difficult. Howard, behind a façade of exuberance, was sensibly worried.

It was in this beginning atmosphere of uneasy gloom that I was to accompany Sir Thomas to a concert in Philadelphia. Howard had called me long distance to impress on me the paramount importance of the event. There had been difficulties with the Philadelphia management. With the utmost diplomacy and a power of persuasion that made him unique on two continents, Howard had hypnotized them into letting bygones be bygones, even such unpardonable ones as the arrival of the conductor fifteen minutes after curtain time, a curtain time that had been on a nationwide hookup!

The present concert was to usher in a new era of peace and commerce between the Philadelphia Orchestra, Sir Thomas Beecham, and ourselves. What was more: the Women's Committee of the orchestra had invited Sir Thomas and the soloist of the occasion, a beautiful British pianist who soon after was to become Lady Beecham, to be their guests of honor at a tea "immediately following the concert." Howard was in heaven. A successful tea party, Sir Thomas showering his irresistible charm and some of his world-famous wisecracks on the women of

Philadelphia—it meant not only that all was forgiven in Philadelphia, it would set a precedent for the country, would redeem the conductor in the good graces of every Women's Committee from coast to coast, and would secure our beefburgers for a long time to come.

All this was vividly on my mind when I entered the Academy of Music on Friday afternoon. There was Sir Thomas, marching across the stage in slow, stately steps, smiling, stopping once in a while to nod at a few musicians, as calm and at ease as if strolling through Regent's Park. In the boxes large clusters of women, easily identified as the members of the committee that bore their name, would soon be ready to drink tea and to serve olive branches as canapés. They smiled, nodded, and clapped their begloved hands. Everybody was happy. All was well.

Sir Thomas stepped onto the little podium and, without a moment's hesitation, hurling his baton towards the drum section, thundered away in the *Star-Spangled Banner*. As always, he was playing it as if leading a troop of red-coated cavalry to battle, roaring a-field in a bright, unrestrained canter, the trumpets blowing, banners waving in the sun. By the time the startled audience had struggled out of their seats, he had already left their faltering voices far behind.

There has been much criticism of Sir Thomas Beecham's playing of the American anthem, which he made sound as if he were rewriting history—ending the War of 1812 in a thundering victory of the British over a dispirited band of Yankees who couldn't even carry a tune. Whenever the point was raised, he explained that the *Star-Spangled Banner* was a war song, not a dirge, damn it all, written during battle, the song of a great nation, and that the printed music carried the tempo indication *With Spirit*. Strange as his galloping tempi sounded at first, I came to like them more than some of the tear-milking performances that were offered by other famous men.

Some of the latter would turn towards the audience, motioning everybody with slow, imploring gestures to rise—their faces torn with patriotic fervor, gripped with passion, literally moisted by tears. The balcony would get its well-measured share of exhortation, the boxes, of course, every last person in the orchestra. At last the stage was set. The conductor would spread out his arms in one last, all-embracing gesture and begin to play. His lips formed words—some words, anyhow—as he hushed players and audience into a senseless *pianissimo molto adagio* while the bombs were bursting in air, only to be able to rise again to his full length, to shake his locks, to look towards heaven as he led them in a mighty *crescendo* to the land of the free and the home of the brave.

Others, as soon as they left the wings and hurried on stage, would point a threatening baton towards a rolling battery of drums. The drums kept thundering, louder and louder, while the conductor made his entrance and the audience staggered to their feet. By the time he had ascended the platform—Eisenhower on a white charger, not Katharski any more—everybody was ready. The baton came down, the drums subsided, Katharski's *Star-Spangled Banner* began to unfurl—ritardandos and diminuendos, flutes juggled on an outstretched palm, the audience singing, a fountain of trombones exploding in red, white, and blue. A magnificent show, a great interpretation, but all it ever hailed proudly, oh so proudly, was Katharski, the great, himself.

Sir Thomas played the anthem loud, fast, and shocking. But he played it straight and beautiful and with exciting reverence. As was true of everything he played, said, or lived, he didn't give a damn what anybody thought about it.

The concert went fine. It had been a lovely program, brilliantly executed, splendidly received. I hurried backstage at once, to escort the conductor to the all-important reception. The ladies were already busily leaving the boxes—tea, peace, and next year's contract for Sir Thomas clearly written on their satisfied backs.

As always, after a performance, Sir Thomas was drippingly wet, his collar a soggy mess, his shirt in a state of dissolution. The reception had been announced for 4:40. It was 4:28. I had a taxi waiting to take him to his hotel where he and his lovely soloist could change and get to the reception in time—the tea party was to take place in the very hotel where they were staying. Everything was just fine.

"Let's have an ice-cream soda," Sir Thomas said as he stepped out on the street, buttoning his topcoat and, graciously, offering his arm to his companion. He turned away from the waiting cab and began walking down Broad Street, congratulating the young lady on her success and urging me to join in the merry conversation. At last he stopped at a drugstore. He looked at the windows and their weird display of cut-rate Americana, said, "This is just the place I have been hoping for," and sailed in.

He helped his companion onto a stool, climbed, a little stiffly, on one himself, and began to study the bill of fare, discussing the various offerings with delight and in intricate detail. At last he decided on a strawberry sundae. The lady thought that was fine. I just had coffee —no sugar, no cream: bitter and black, I began to feel, was the drink befitting the hour.

The soda jerker seemed fascinated by the strange apparition: a drippingly wet old gentleman accompanied by a gorgeously dressed blonde perching there in broad daylight. He began to compose the sundaes with infinite care and elaboration, pausing from time to time to listen, spellbound, to the comments of admiration Sir Thomas addressed to him in magnificent prose. By the time he had finished what must have been his supreme masterwork, adding a final layer of chocolate sauce with an almost sensual tenderness and putting the dishes with a sweeping gesture before the illustrious couple, it was four thirty-nine.

There are no words to describe the ensuing eleven minutes. Never have I seen a man consuming food with a greater amount of joy, relaxation, and utter peace with the world. From time to time I rested my eyes on him with a look that would have moved a rock—but to no avail. The last sip ascended through a crumpling straw at 4:50. Sir Thomas got up, extended a gallant arm to the lady, and marched through the store, Sir John Falstaff benevolently walking through an honor guard of Dutch Masters and rubber articles at half price.

When we arrived at the hotel, the lady retired to her room, making it clear that she would be ready in ten minutes. Sir Thomas, after having urged her to take her time, sat down and poured himself a drink. Then he began telling me about his experiences with the symphony orchestra in Melbourne.

The lady, at last, returned. She was quite ready now to go but was first asked to sit down and have a drink. This she did. The lady sat down, at five fourteen, to have a drink with us.

I thought I would never see the moment (but I saw it at 5:28) when Sir Thomas excused himself and retired to finish his toilet. Soon I heard him whistling gay tunes under the shower. Another ten minutes went down the drain towards the eternal river of time and he emerged— clean, dry, in a flashy cutaway, a gray tie loosely flowing from his immaculate collar. He plucked a carnation from a vase, put it in his buttonhole, and turned to his companion.

"Let us go and join the ladies," he said.

The telephone had an evil sound.

"Is this Sir Thomas Beecham's room?" a dowagery voice said.

I couldn't talk. But the voice didn't wait for an answer.

"Will you please tell Sir Thomas that we are all going home," it said.

Sir Thomas had come over. He took the phone and listened. Then I saw his freshly showered forehead redden.

"Madame," he said loudly and clearly, "this is a social outrage."

I looked at the big clock on the mantel.

It was 5:43.

Howard, when he came home from his trip, seemed not quite so crushed by the Philadelphia disaster as I had anticipated. He didn't really seem to care so much any more—he the most elaborate carer I had ever seen! For the first time signs of strain appeared on his ever-cheerful face. His booking trip, he reported, had been a great disappointment.

He couldn't figure it out. He had a fine list of brilliant artists. He certainly knew all about the business—but something, somewhere, was wrong. Oh, people had been wonderful. He got offers to spend the night, urgent requests to come back and see us at any time, assurances that we will let you know as soon as possible. He brought home snapshots and souvenirs and memories of southern belles who had driven him to his train and who never before had been subjected to the charm of a former lieutenant in the First Hungarian Honvéd Brigade.

But he didn't bring home the bacon. He had lined up a few college dates, music club recitals with plenty of prestige and little cash in half a dozen towns that were separated by half a continent and by prohibitive railroad fares. The Tuesday Morning Musicale in Oklahoma City was interested in our harpsichordist and the Provo summer school gave some thought to our chamber orchestra. But there was an enormous number of events all over the country—thousands of regular concert courses, symphony orchestras engaging soloists galore, brilliant dates with brilliant fees—where he had been unable to break in.

Then an event occurred, insignificant and small on the surface, but full of meaning if properly understood. And Howard was no fool. He understood.

He had been particularly persistent in his efforts to secure a permanent place in the Hall of Fame for a young singer, a fine Canadian baritone named Hugh Mac-Donald. Howard had discovered him singing in a church in the upper Bronx. He loved him like a son, believed in his ultimate success, and worked for him like a beaver. He was not after quick profits in Hugh MacDonald's case. He had even gone so far—an unheard-of violation of ethics in the concert manager's code—as to advance to him the money needed for folders, photographs, throwaways, three-sheets, press books, and all the other hokum that sits, an unwanted but always hungry guest, at a concert artist's shaky table.

Finally Howard introduced him to Sir Thomas Beecham, who gave him a handwritten letter of recommendation. It was reproduced in facsimile and mailed to every prospective buyer of a baritone.

Never have I seen a happier, a more grateful man than Hugh MacDonald. He insisted on signing a five-year exclusive contract with us. Howard was his friend, his benefactor, his father, his redeemer. The contract—five years' exclusive representation for concerts, radio, opera, television, records in this or any other world—was signed with flashlights blazing and glasses clinking all over Fifty-seventh Street.

Three weeks later Hugh called up and asked for an appointment. All he wanted was "a little chat."

"I wonder what he wants to chat about," Howard said with a melancholy face.

The next day Hugh MacDonald came up to the office for his little chat. There was a lot of small talk—weather talk, health talk, looking-fine talk—with Hugh writhing uncomfortably on his chair, looking out of the window and down at his shoes, and Howard looking straight at him and firing away in exuberant sadism with tales about fabulous prospects and all the wonderful things he and Hugh would accomplish together during the next four years and forty-nine weeks. At last Hugh couldn't take it any more. The little chat began.

One of the Big Concert Agencies in New York—there are only two and, by St. Libel, I am not going to say which one—had received the facsimile of Sir Thomas

Beecham's letter in the mail. A few days later, Hugh chatted on, the Big Concert Agency had called him on the phone. Why didn't he drop in one of these days, maybe Wednesday morning, let's say half-past ten, for a little chat.

"There is nothing wrong with that," Hugh said, looking at Howard, and Howard said, "No, there is nothing wrong with that," and he looked at Hugh and Hugh looked out of the window and nobody said anything for a little while.

When Hugh got up to the Big Concert Agency he met in the waiting room the accompanist who always played for him at auditions. Had an appointment at the same time, ten-thirty, Wednesday. Strange coincidence, wasn't it?

"Very strange," said Howard, leaning back in his chair, keeping his puszta-brown eyes fixed on the wretched singer.

So they began chatting, Hugh and the accompanist, and then a man came out and said Gee, isn't that nice, you know each other and why don't you come in for a little chat and as long as you both are here what about a little music.

Hugh sang; a few people drifted in, quite a few, in fact, a dozen or so, and they all stood around and listened. It was quite an elaborate affair. And when he stopped after half an hour they all came over and shook hands, my, they were real nice. It turned out that they were all bookers and organizers and travelers and press agents and program directors and regional advisers and vice-presidents and chairmen of the board for the Big Concert Agency—just dropping in by accident. Nice, wasn't it?

"Nice," said Howard. "Very, very nice."

One of them told Hugh that they had sixty men on the road. Imagine, sixty men traveling and booking artists all year round. This fellow worked out of Tulsa, just think of it, working out of Tulsa all year round, Hugh said, casting a guarded eye over the single room that was our office and Howard and me and Miss Bromberger who were its only inhabitants.

Howard looked at me and at Miss Bromberger and then *he* looked out of the window, and Hugh didn't look at his shoes any more but looked straight at Howard.

Well, he continued, afterwards somebody had asked him to step in his office. It was such a happy coincidence—they were just looking for a young baritone—and they all liked him and would be happy to take him on.

When he told them that he had just signed a five-year contract with us, the man was terribly embarrassed. Gee, the man said, isn't that too bad—why, we will never interfere with your commitments, a contract is a contract. Isn't it a shame, though? We really needed a young baritone—Miss O'Hara, where is that letter from Madame Paroni, she writes me about one of her pupils, a young baritone from New Orleans, call her up and ask her to bring him in tomorrow.

A little later, while Hugh was waiting for the elevator,

the man from Tulsa crossed over from the gentlemen's lounge.

"It's really too bad," he said. "We all liked you. Why, in my own little territory I could book you for twenty dates, just like that." He snapped his fingers. The red light at the elevator flashed on. As Hugh had one foot already in the car, the man from Tulsa spoke once more.

"Why don't you see what you can do about it?" he said.

The next year Hugh MacDonald sang twenty dates in the Tulsa territory. He also sang eighty-nine more in the territories of fourteen other provincial lords of the Big Concert Agency. He was where he wanted to be. He had become a cogwheel in the mightiest music-producing machine in the world.

Howard—Hunyadi again—was selling insurance. I was back where I belonged.

RHEINGOLD

The mightiest music-producing machine in the world is operated by two giants, the Fafner and the Fasolt of music in America: Columbia Artists Management and National Concert and Artists Corporation. It is a sparkling maze of wealth, glamour, and strength, solidly built on the rock of Manhattan, where it is hardest, sturdiest, and most likely to last. It turns out some ten thousand concerts in two thousand cities, towns, and villages every year.

Hundreds of little cogwheels such as Hugh MacDonald rotate in its mighty body. Sixty-eight well-oiled sopranos, twelve contraltos, twenty-seven tenors, thirty-six baritones can be seen and heard, grinding forever around the clock. Fifty-four pianists clatter noisily. Twenty-nine violinists are being pushed around and around and around. Seven cellists hum in the lower registers.

A lavish assortment of harpists, guitarists, harmonica virtuosos, two-piano teams, dance groups, violists, conductors move restlessly and with unfailing precision at their designated spots. Theremists can be seen spinning dizzily, grand-opera quintets, the Don Cossacks as well as the original Don Cossacks, marimba dervishes, bel canto trios, carolers, balladeers, twentieth-century minstrels, boy choirs from Norway, Vienna, and Columbus, Ohio, Hindu dancers, opera companies, the De Paur Infantry Chorus, the Sadler's Wells Ballet.

When one of the parts, big or small, begins to show signs of wear, age, or independence, it is thrown out, mercilessly, and replaced by a spare called in from the factories in Town Hall or Carnegie Hall where replacements are turned out on forever rotating assembly lines. More than one hundred debutants come off the Town Hall plant alone in a single year; they are tested by the operating giants, rejected most of them, a few selected to take their place in the machine. Cog 181 is junked. Cog 181a begins to rotate. Nobody notices the difference.

The machine keeps on going, puffing, whirling, steaming, sweating, turning out music, the patent medicine that cures all aches, pains, and worries, beautifully bottled, packaged, labeled, and crated, endorsed by famous authorities and priced far above its actual value. The trains are waiting, the planes, the cars—and the wonder drug is off to cities and sticks, to streamlined auditoriums and musty barns, across the mountains and into the deserts, to the waiting, paying multitudes. Three million

Americans have been welded together into one big, happy family of contented customers by the biggest merchandising idea that has ever revolutionized the concert field and completely changed the musical scene: the Organized Audience Plan.

I can hear the clatter of the machine while I am sitting here, many blocks away. It never stops, it is always present wherever you listen to music in America. Even Major and Minor seem affected by it. Maybe there is a career for them, performing love duets in seventeen towns in the Tulsa territory, two hundred dollars a date, after commission and expenses.

Don't fly off yet, fellows. Tulsa is far—and it says here "after commission and expenses." Careful now. Move over here first. Let me tell you what it is all about and how it happened. It's all so young, so sudden, so very big for its age. Just thirty years ago there was no Fasolt, no Fafner, nothing.

Chicago, 1921. The scene: the office of Harry P. Harrison, president of the Redpath Chautauqua and Lyceum Bureau. The man behind the desk—tall, bony, healthy, but slightly worried-looking—Mr. Harry P. Harrison himself.

Why should Harry P. Harrison look worried this fine morning? For many years he has been organizing chautauquas and has sold his colorful combinations of vaudeville, circus, theater, religion, and adult education to hundreds of communities. What wonderful, rich pageants they were—how dull and barren are our own days where an hour with Milton Berle on a ridiculous screen in the living-room corner has replaced all the excitement, the noise, the smells, the blaring bands, the good-fellowship, the thundering speeches, the corn and glamour of seven days, yes, seven days of continuous entertainment—three different shows each day—twenty-one shows for three dollars and less.

In their heyday they played to five million people during a single summer. Five thousand would stream into a town of five hundred population to participate in the event. Factories would close, paying their workers full wages for the week of the chautauqua. Thousands of people participated in the gargantuan shows—tent stakers and promoters, actors and singers, revivalists and musicians. Complete operettas (Victor Herbert's *Sweethearts* was one of the favorites on the circuit) and tear-milking plays alternated with lectures. William Jennings Bryan, the greatest among them, delivered for two years his famous oration "Brother or Brute," twice a day "uplifting the people through the bigness of heart and soul and impressing them with his great honesty of purpose."

Madame Ernestine Schumann-Heink had come to sing on chautauquas between appearances at the Metropolitan Opera, sandwiched in between the Dunbar Singing Bell Ringers and Baby Harold Chester with the Musical Moores. There were junior chautauquas, health pageants, cartoonists, vaudeville. And there was the Wolverine Quartet Doubling in Brass.

One of the four Wolverines was a thin, energetic, nervous-looking man who sang baritone and played the bugle. His name was Ward French.

Name sounds familiar, Minor?

It should. There isn't a pigeon in all America hasn't heard it. Bugler French is today chairman of the board of Columbia Artists Management in New York.

How come?

Now you just be quiet, and listen.

What a business the chautauquas had been! At their peak, shortly before the first World War, they played for almost ten thousand communities. Harrison's Redpath was only one of thirty agencies booking chautauquas and lyceums throughout the country. Two hundred and nine different sets of tents, crews, and equipment, 175 different programs were simultaneously in operation.

But to Harry Harrison, in 1921, all this had become memories only of a happier past. Business was falling off rapidly. He couldn't blame it on a lack of traditional attractions or on his bookers who went around as busily and persuasive as ever. Maybe he should have read the prophetic words of a contemporary observer—words that should be remembered at all times by everyone who thinks he knows what the public wants. "The chautauqua," this wise man said, "gives the public what *it thinks the public wants* and the public takes it, which makes money for the chautauqua, and thus spares the chautauqua any need of conceiving and carrying out a program with more specific gravity. *But it is also possible that the public would also be found to want—that is, be willing to pay for—something better. Nobody knows, and certainly the chautauqua makes no effort to find out.*"

Harrison had to find out. This had become a different country, all of a sudden. A new generation was growing up in a changed spiritual, cultural, political, and social climate. The old mother-heaven-home formula that had inspired their parents and swept their grandparents off their feet had lost its magic. The people, indeed, wanted "something better." The chautauqua and the happy days it stood for had come to an end. A big entertainment industry was about to be wiped out, completely and forever.

What would take its place? This was to be the age of radio. Music began coming over the air waves, entering, for the first time, millions of American homes. A transformation of the taste, the spiritual needs of the people was under way. Symphony orchestras began to sprout in towns that had never been willing to devote a penny of their citizens' money, an hour of their citizens' time, to music. Music schools were founded and lavishly endowed. Bands, organized in every high school, captured the imagination of millions. Huge factories began to turn out instruments.

Harrison decided to start the Redpath Music Bureau, an agency devoted to the dispensation of musical artists. Miss Dema Harshbarger, who had booked chautauquas

for many successful years, was put in charge. It turned
out to be a momentous decision.

Miss Harshbarger went about the booking of Harold
Bauer, Albert Spalding, and Léon Rothier with the same
enthusiasm that had gone into the dispensation of sea
lions and revival meetings. But the going was tough.
Every concert was a gamble—a gamble on rain or sleet or
a warehouse fire that would, at the last minute, disas-
trously interfere with the box office. Local guarantors and
promoters lost money. When the booker came back to
the same town the second time, there weren't any guarantors and promoters left.

And so we see Miss Harshbarger plead with a group of
reluctant citizens of Battle Creek, Michigan, to under-
write $750—so that a famous violinist could come and
play in the town. It wasn't a lot of money for the violinist.
By the time he paid his commission to Redpath, who sold
him to Battle Creek, and to the New York manager who
sold him to Redpath, and traveling expenses for himself
and his accompanist, and the accompanist's fee, and folders and programs and the press agent and the personal
representative, and the photographer who took pictures
when he boarded the train in New York, and the photographer who took pictures when he left the train in
Battle Creek, and ads in the trade papers so that the
trade papers would print the photographs—just remember all that, fellows, before flying off to Tulsa!—by that
time there wasn't much left. But the citizens in Battle
Creek didn't look at it that way. They had been hooked

before. Battle Creek, they felt, could do without a $750 violinist from New York.

It was then that the spirit descended on Miss Harshbarger and changed her from a frustrated booker for a dying industry into a mighty instrument of history. Let us form a club in this town, she improvised with inspired tongue, a club of real music lovers, a concert organization where every member pays dues—five dollars, let's say, per year. That isn't much, is it? Well, if you and your friends and the friends of your friends all get together we should find a few hundred people in this town willing to join up. If you get five hundred members you'll have twenty-five hundred dollars in the bank. You can engage enough artists to fill a whole concert course, and there won't be any risk—none at all. If the members don't show up for the concert, and would rather go see the warehouse fire instead—it will be their loss, not yours.

That's how it all began.

For the next few days telephones rang all over Battle Creek. Miss Harshbarger stayed on to conduct the campaign, to advise, to help organize a "non-profit concert organization." After a week had passed, nine hundred people had signed up. The $750 violinist and four other Redpath artists had been engaged. Overwhelmed and a little dazed, Miss Harshbarger departed to report to the boss. He said that was fine. He didn't think much of the idea. He had grown up in a different world.

There were others, however, who had better ears and finer noses. The scene now shifts to the town of Wanatah, Indiana, a few days after the dramatic events in Battle Creek had taken their predestined course. It is Saturday. In a hotel lobby a thin, energetic, nervous-looking man: Ward French, formerly baritone and bugler, now a little thinner, a little more nervous, a chautauqua booker for Redpath, and a very unhappy, very frustrated booker indeed. For weeks now *Götterdämmerung* had stared him, bleak, in the face.

Wanatah had not been different. He had spent five days trying to get a booking, and he knew he would never get one. And now a week end in Wanatah! In desperation he remembered, suddenly, that he had an old roommate from college days in a town near by. He checked out and left. The town he was heading for—there are things between heaven and earth!—was Battle Creek, Michigan.

Here is the sequence of events for the next few hours:

(a) Booker French arrives in Battle Creek. Roommate is delighted. They settle down on front porch to while away the day.

(b) Roommate, feeling obliged to make conversation, yawns out the intelligence that "we will have a few concerts here next year, starting with a piano recital by Harold Bauer."

(c) Booker French stops rocking chair.

(d) Roommate relates that "some woman was down here," organized the Civic Music Association of Battle Creek, made roommate vice-president.

(e) Booker kicks over rocking chair, rushes off for Chicago, enters Harry Harrison's office, and shouts: "This is the answer to the concert business." Harry P. Harrison asks him to take it easy.

This is the story related by ex-booker French. There is no reason to doubt its veracity, although it sounds a little like Frederick the Great addressing his officers on the day he had declared war on Maria Theresa of Austria and dismissing the meeting with the immortal words: "And now, gentlemen, let us be off for the Seven Years' War."

The years to come were indeed war years for Ward French. Harrison remained cool towards "the answer to the concert business." Another man, O. O. Botroff, formerly a tent staker on the Redpath circuit, caught on to the idea and tried to organize a chain of towns under the new plan. Samuel Insull, for a little time, took an interest in it. French went around, at his own, limited expense, preaching the new doctrine, explaining, expostulating, succeeding once in a while, failing mostly. The big New York concert managers looked with suspicion on the unorthodox scheme. Artists refused to co-operate. As the depression began to sweep the land, the end of the Organized Audience Plan seemed only a matter of a few paydays.

And then, when things looked bleakest, in 1931, there was a knock at French's dilapidated door, sharp, commanding, the knock of a giant. It was a messenger from New York. Would Mr. Ward French please come and see Mr. Arthur Judson, president of Columbia Concerts Corporation.

A few hours later French was on the train. He knew that he would never return.

This was it.

In the music room of the New York Public Library one can find a little booklet, attractively bound in blue cloth, printed on heavy, expensive, glossy paper. It is called *Columbia Concerts Corporation Artists Almanac, 1931.* It announces the formation of Columbia Concerts, lists the six powerful concert managers who had pooled their financial resources, staffs, and brains to form the new combine and—on eighty-nine power-packed pages—the brilliant lists of artists they controlled. The six were the *crème de la crème* of American concert business: F. C. Coppicus, Evans & Salter, the old firm of Hansel and Jones, the Metropolitan Music Bureau, Wolfsohn, the oldest concert manager in America, and Arthur Judson, formerly a concert violinist and now the driving power behind the new trust and its first president.

"This corporation claims," the almanac fanfares, "that it is able to supply all concert demands, however great or modest, of every club, school, or college, organization or individual entrepreneur, and the formidable roster of talent which makes up the content of this book is the evidence supporting this claim. The book was issued in spite of the depression. In the task of recovery the solace and the inspiration of music will play its accustomed part, and the artists listed in this book, couriers of that lovely muse, are ready and eager to spread the message of cheer and joy to the four corners of this great land."

The task of recovery and the spreading of messages of cheer and joy was to be greatly facilitated by the fortunate fact that Columbia Concerts was owned by the Columbia Broadcasting System and its ninety-two stations, ready and eager to administer the solace and inspiration of music mainly if not exclusively through those couriers of the lovely muse who were on the lists of Columbia Concerts.

And if all this wasn't enough to usher in the millennium—the Columbia millennium—Ward French, the man who had known the answer to the concert business for so many years, was now on his way to New York! "The time has come," Columbia Concerts declared, "to streamline the advancement of artists' careers by such corporation methods as have long been used in the distribution of refrigerators." A chilly simile to apply to the couriers of the lovely muse and the joy and cheer they were to spread to the four corners of this great land—but similes were not on Ward French's mind as he paced, restlessly, the corridors of the train.

This, at last, was his vindication. What would be more dazzling a plan, more promising an adventure than to combine the wealth, the staff, the facilities, and the brilliant lists of artists which all were at Columbia's disposal with his own grandiose dreams of organizing audiences not in tens but in hundreds, in thousands of Battle Creeks? Who would be able to resist such sweeping power? Which artist would dare to stay aside, which local entrepreneur would refuse to surrender, which audience not be willing to be organized? None.

And it all came through. President French of Community Concert Service, "a division of Columbia Concerts Corporation," soon had sixty organizers on the road. Concert courses were organized by the ton, by the carload, by the battleship.

While all this went on in Steinway Hall, the National Broadcasting Company formed their own concert agency, the National Concert and Artists Corporation. O. O. Botroff, the former tent staker for Redpath, was called in to supervise their own brand of community concerts under the organized audience plan—the Civic Concert Series. Between the two of them, Community and Civic have organized the incredible total of two thousand towns in the United States and Canada under the Battle Creek system.

When a frown from the Federal Communications Commission and a threatening suit under the antitrust laws forced the big radio chains to cut their ties with their concert bureaus, no harm was done. The Organized Audience Plan was established. The biggest music-producing machine in the world was working in streamlined, gleaming, undisturbed perfection. It still is.

The power assembled in such a machine is staggering. A nod from Fafner or Fasolt can grant or deny an artist one hundred concert dates in a season, can be the difference between success and oblivion, wealth or starvation. To make an independent career without playing the circuit is possible only for the very great who have outgrown even the all-embracing power of the two giants, who can choose their own dates and dictate their own fees—or for those who don't care, who make music for music's sake and are satisfied with whatever the world of independent intellectualism can provide for them, which isn't too much.

Fasolt and Fafner don't like to hear such summaries of facts. They are nervous giants, allergic to criticism. Anyone snooping around the cave is suspected of being after the gold, and is hit at with open letters and similar clumsy clubs. They like to think of themselves as national institutions, as pioneers who selflessly give their lives so that beauty may reign in Topeka. They are deeply hurt when a House Judiciary Subcommittee wants to investigate them for alleged monopolistic practices; and when Virgil Thomson accuses them of contaminating the taste of American audiences by censoring their artists' programs in a most arbitrary fashion and of standardizing the repertory at the level of the least cultivated cities in the chain, they break out in tears.

Yet the fact is clear and undeniable: concert business in America today is overwhelmingly governed by the supreme power built up by the Big Two. It has been acquired in a quite legitimate way, to be sure, exactly as predicted: by the successful methods that have brought millions of refrigerators into the American home.

The Big Two influence, decisively, the lives of hundreds of artists, the musical fare of millions of listeners.

They determine what artists the people in two thousand towns will hear; even if—on paper—"any person appearing before the public can be presented by any local Community and Civic association," at least 85 per cent of the artists appearing there with any regularity are from the lists of the Big Two. They determine to a very large extent the music these artists will perform, convinced that they, and they alone, know what is good for the people, for the artists, and for music in general, or, as they themselves word it much more eloquently: "what the public wants badly enough to pay for."

And yet, in spite of all that has been said against the machine and the two giants who gather gold, tears, the bones of the frustrated, the wilted flowers of hope in their interminable caves, big and dangerous as they are, they have taken their rightful place on the ever-changing scene of music in America. They started to cultivate the deserts when smaller men failed. It is quite true when they claim that they have provided music for millions at nominal cost. It is true when they claim that they have not only given their huge audiences the great stars of our time but have also enabled hundreds of young artists to get a hearing in communities who never heard their names before and would not have given them a chance to prove their worth or their failure in the cold light of experience without that gentle but irresistible pressure from the front office.

With all their faults, their politics, their musical censorship, with all the dangers that come with an overgrowth of power in any field of human relations, they have done service not only to themselves but to music. They were an important link in the chain. Without them, music would not be what it is today in America.

What will the future be?

Is it really only a few decades since chautauquas played to ten thousand American towns? Where have the mighty gone? Mute are the bugles of the Wolverines, dark the fireworks in the nocturnal skies, blown away the tents, the merry caravans, the laughter, the cheer, the crowds. Even the echoes of yesterday's music have faded away.

This is a big and restless land. "The chautauqua," the wise man had said, "gives the public what it thinks the public wants . . . But it is also possible that the public would also be found to want—that is, be willing to pay for —something better." If one would just replace the word chautauqua by Modern Concert Biz. . . .

Mightily pounds the machine—but mightier is the pounding of the human heart. The thirst for beauty can never be stilled from all the wonder bottles that come over the assembly lines, by all the hucksters in the medicine show.

Light and clouds change forever. Over the iron rhythm of the machine I can hear the strains of a different music, lovely and free, falling like a gentle, steady rain on the fertile soil of the land.

Be off now, pigeons. Back to your window.

Can't you hear the celestial voice, lovely and free, coming through the mist? Here comes my ladylove.

Be gone, we want to be alone.

All the letters on my table, the posters on my walls, the pictures in my drawers, the memories in my heart belong to her. She wasn't with me for a long time, and sometimes I thought I would never see her again. But now she has returned.

I can hear her voice and see her face again.

GIRL

WITH

A HUNDRED FACES

My ladylove is the most beautiful girl in the world. She is *la femme à cent têtes*—the girl with a hundred heads, a hundred faces. She has the most beautiful names in the world—hundreds of them: Carmencita, Mélisande, Cherubin, Pamina, Mimi, Maria Ehrenreich, Fidelio.

She is a queen, my ladylove, a gipsy, a doll, a saint, a warrior, a beautiful, maddening bitch. She has thousands of dresses, pearls, crowns, furs, helmets, and sparkling tiaras, lovely soft muffs, hats, shoes, and scarfs. Stars glow in her hair, her hands carry daggers and precious stones, roses of gentle silver breathing Persia's most exquisite scents, chalices filled with the elixirs of love and of death.

Gods and villains follow her, harlequins, mermaids, giants and limping dwarfs, dark slaves from Ethiopia, horses, elephants, and doves, Satan himself with feather and sword. Night owls sing her praises and nightingales, golden cockerels flap their wings as she passes, the silver voice of the forest's most precious bird climbs through the treetops to guide her. When she smiles, wine pours from the innkeeper's sign, swords glow in mighty oaks, flames and roaring waters lose their evil threat, and the mountains begin to glow in a wall of greeting fire.

There is no joy like hers and no despair, no laughter and no heartbreaking tear, no innocence and no guilt, no sacrifice, no tenderness, no burning hate, and no all-consuming love. There is no other woman in the world like my ladylove.

I have always been in love with her, ever since I met her first in the little rococo opera house in my home town in Germany. I was a boy then. Her name was Martha. Soon we met again, at the same enchanted spot. The first gusts of spring burst open the doors and Sieglinde, my love, was swept away towards happiness and destruction.

A little later Bruno Walter came to our town to conduct a festival. What I had known of my love appeared feeble and pale now that her real beauty had been revealed. Pamina, Constanza, Fiordiligi, Susanna—the light they were walking on, the passion, the drama, the gripping enchantment of the music that made their hearts beat, their outcries real, their songs the very quintessence of love, fear, faith. It was music that could never be matched by any music I had heard or would ever hear in a concert hall. It was the mirrored reflection of life itself. The unique combination of drama, music, dance, movement, color, sound, and action—there was nothing like it in any other field of the arts.

The great conductor came back once more, a few years later, to make us shiver with Elektra's dark hatred, Salome's vibrating hysteria, the wine, the laughter, the lust of Sophie, Octavian, Bichette.

I was lost forever.

Soon fate, unpredictable and kind, brought us together still closer. We entered into an intimacy I had never dared hope for standing up there on the fourth balcony in the little theater, in the dark niches of the "Olympus," following the score with a sickly flashlight while down below, far in the distance, small and very remote, Louise went to her merry doom and Mimi coughed her tormented soul into the icy Parisian night. Fate took me by the hand and guided me down from olympus—into the parquet, the orchestra, even backstage. I had become a professional. Louise came very close; and as I was sitting right by her feet, knowing her name, her age, her agent, death seemed to lose some of its horrors as Mimi, rose-cheeked in spite of a heavy make-up, gave up her ghost in E-flat major.

At the age of twenty-three I had become head of the operatic department of Universal Edition, a big, progressive music publishing house in Vienna. Ernst Krenek, Darius Milhaud, Leos Janaček, Jaromir Weinberger, Alban Berg, Kurt Weill, and scores of other composers were under my juvenile, unbelieving wings. For fifteen wonderful years, from 1923 to 1938, I lived in the midst of the great operatic movement that made Europe vibrate with activity, daring experiments, a sweeping belief in the impossible, the unorthodox, the new.

There was Alban Berg and his *Wozzeck*, right at the beginning. I was in the Berlin Opera House on December 14, 1925, when the curtain went up for the first time on one of the great masterpieces of modern art.

Berg had seen the play by Georg Büchner—a fragment only of a play left unfinished by the poet, who had died, almost a boy, after a few flamboyant, explosively creative years, a hundred years ago—and was at once deeply gripped by the powerful story and its pitiful people. *Wozzeck* was as unique an operatic libretto as was *Carmen*—it is, indeed, a German *Carmen*, with an identical background of primitive passion, jealousy, infidelity, and murder. Wozzeck himself, the poor, dumb soldier, is a dark, nordic Don José, Marie the Carmen of a German *Kleinstadt*, the *Tambourmajor* a strutting Escamillo in a Prussian uniform. Lillas Pastia's inn is a dreary *Biergarten*: no sparkling manzanilla makes the blood flow faster—the drunks are heavy with cheap beer and poisonous schnaps. The *seguidilla* isn't danced here. The castanets are silent. Heavy move the dancers, clumsily swaying under a cold, dark moon. The soldiers don't wear the bright yellow of the Dragoons, helmets sparkling in the rays of the southern sun—they are anonymous numbers in anonymous garb. Yet the story is the same. . . .

Berg was deeply attracted to the world of little people that inspired him to write the most important and most successful opera of his generation. Many years later, after the work had been established, a small incident occurred that made the composer's deep passion for the people in his opera touchingly clear. The Austrian Tabac Monopoly had issued two new cigarettes named after operas: one they called Jonny in honor of Ernst Krenek's *Jonny Spielt Auf*—a cigarette packaged and flavored like an American cigarette and destined to please the taste of visiting dollar spenders. The other one, Heliane, was an expensive luxury product, named after a luscious operatic score by a local composer. Berg (a passionate chain smoker himself) had one of his pupils write a long, carefully stylized letter to the manufacturers, suggesting that their cheapest cigarette, the one only the very poor would buy (and which they mostly broke open and smoked in their worn-out pipes), should be named Wozzeck. He never received a reply.

Today Wozzeck has its place next to *Pelléas et Mélisande;* not a "popular" opera, yet accepted, all over the world, as a work of indisputable, towering stature. But on that night there were fist fights, challenges shouted across the orchestra seats and from the loges, deriding laughter, boos, and shrill whistles that threatened, for some time, to overpower the small but, at last, victorious group of determined believers. Did we who battled so

valiantly, shouted and clapped and stayed on till the
lights went out in the house and the iron curtain descended, did we "understand" so new, so revolutionary,
so great a work? Maybe a few of us did—but most of us
didn't. What of it? There is an inner ear, an invisible
antenna that doesn't register the weak voices of the rule
books, the subterranean rustle of counterpoint moles, the
spinstery outcries of parallel fifths, but is touched, magically, by beauty, power, strength, the thundering step of
a giant.

The violent contrasts of opinion continued the next
morning, and for days and weeks to come, in the press.
High praise, humble recognition of the greatness of the
work and the singular significance of its creator on one
side—foaming, almost hysterical condemnation on the
other. We printed it all in a little booklet, *Wozzeck and
the Berlin Music Critics*, leaving the decision of who
would be proven right or wrong to the inescapable judgment of history.

Recently I heard *Wozzeck* again—in Carnegie Hall in
New York. A refined, slightly blasé, by no means revolutionary public followed the work with breathless attention. At the end of the stirring performance a tremendous
ovation rocked the walls of the noble hall. When I went
home that night I looked through my old papers. There
was the little booklet, faded its cover, brittle the pages—
still exhaling the trembling excitement, the almost reli-
gious belief that had shaken us when we put it together,
a quarter of a century ago! "If this is not a deliberate

swindle, my name will be Moses Sewersmell," one critic wrote. "When I left the theater I felt that I wasn't leaving a public place dedicated to the arts but a public lunatic asylum. There isn't a trace of melody in Berg's music. In the orchestra one hears but the noises of a complete zoo. I consider Berg a musical mountebank. But one has to go even further. Unheard-of events ask for new methods. One has to ask oneself seriously whether musical activities cannot be criminal. We are faced, in the realm of music, with a capital offense. There remains only one hope: that the public will be unwilling to take a seat in the Augean stable of Berg's art."

There were additional smells from the sewers—and in the days to come more violence. Even politics were injected into the battle. It took years till the smoke had cleared and the work and the man became plainly visible to all. But there were also many who immediately recognized the event—many of the brilliant writers on music of the day, conductors, artists all over the world. There are a few sentences in the forgotten little pamphlet that describe in moving words the magic power of the spirit. They go far beyond the single case of Alban Berg, of *Wozzeck*, of the distant events around the stormy première of 1925. I'd like to rescue them from oblivion.

"Berlin became the place for a great deed and its far-reaching consequences," says a letter from an unknown observer to a Viennese newspaper, printed in the opening pages of the pamphlet. "I am referring to Alban Berg's *Wozzeck*. I, myself, have only a remote association with

music. It isn't given to me—and it can't be forced. Maybe
that makes it easier for me to observe an important event
from the periphery with a certain measure of objectivity.

"What has happened? A composer whose name had
not penetrated beyond a small circle of experts comes
from Vienna to Berlin to have his work performed. The
next day the *Kulturwelt* knows the name of Alban Berg.
We feel, at once, that a new brilliant light has risen and
will be visible around the globe. Once again we see the
rare and, for its rareness, doubly heart-warming spectacle
of the materialization of a great spiritual force. An artistic
deed of greatness and sincerity and high, undiluted purpose has only to be done in order to conquer the hearts
of man.

"Such a deed has its effects far beyond the circle of
those actually participating in it. A mysterious magic is at
work. Many who are quite remote from the event hear of
it and are, at once, strangely moved. They do not know
why. In the mysterious workings of a higher life the event
itself is not the most significant part: more important is
its strange radiation. Suddenly there is a circle on the
water, growing and growing. The scope of artistic communication has been widened. People are grateful and
strangely elated.

"In the hearts of man is a deep sense of justice. Love
and gratitude are offered the few who push further the
frontiers of the spiritual world, and even to us, the distant
observers of so magnificent an event, it is happiness to be
allowed to pay our respect."

Today, in retrospect, these words, written immediately after the first performance of Wozzeck, long before the lasting significance of the event had been established, seem touching, prophetic words. The mysterious, permanent radiation of Berg's work is as singular as was the overwhelming radiation of his own personality. I remember him so well—the very tall, slightly stooped man with the beautiful Oscar Wildean head, the elegant, aristocratic Austrian accent, the earthy humor, the gentle, kindly soul. What an imposing couple they were, the tall, dark man and his tall, blond, very beautiful wife who dressed slightly old-fashionedly and had her magnificent tresses wound around her proud head in princely, almost imperial fashion.

Many times I have been in their smallish apartment in a Viennese suburb, close by the lavish gardens of Schönbrunn castle, where Berg liked to go for long solitary walks. They spent the summers in a house they owned at one of Austria's innumerable lakes. Both homes were filled with the unmistakable signs of culture of the highest degree, the tradition of generations: every picture had some special meaning, every book had its place in the spiritual aura of the home. He had many friends and liked them around. At once he attracted attention, commanded respect. But of the few really great men I have known, he was by far the most human, the least forbidding, the most modest, easygoing, friendly one.

He was fond of the mysteries of figures. One of his ancestors (the family traced their origins back to Ger-

many, to Nürnberg with its old houses and churches and
torture chambers) must have been an alchemist, very
close to ancient formulas and the dark secrets of black
magic. Strange coincidences, mysterious alignments of
figures in time and space were ever present in his never-
resting mind. It all emerged again in the incredibly complicated yet simple and logical formulas and proportions
of his scores.

The figure 23 had special significance. The first attack
of the asthma that plagued him all his life had occurred
on the twenty-third of July, 1900. He wrote important
letters on a twenty-third and pointed out that many decisive letters had arrived, mysteriously, on a twenty-third.
He even timed the completion of his works so that at
least the first sketch would be ready on the magic date.
The *Violin Concerto* was completed on the twenty-third
of July, 1935. During his fatal illness he was always aware
of the decisive importance of the date. He fell into a
coma on the twenty-third of December, 1935, and died
only an hour after the fateful day had passed.

The figure again appeared as the name of a fighting
little avant-garde magazine that Willi Reich, Berg's pupil,
friend, and biographer, published in Vienna for several
years. Berg had suggested the name "*23*" for the magazine
and drew himself a symbolic sketch for the cover. This
time the figure took on a new significance: 23 was also
the number of the famous paragraph in the Austrian press
law that gave anyone the right to demand a correction of
news items he considered wrong in facts. "*23*" now be-

came the magazine that corrected many wrongs and attacked lustily in many fields of music.

That the "new brilliant light" which the unknown observer discovered on the spiritual horizon after Wozzeck had first been performed in 1925 should still shine, more brilliant and brighter as every year passes, even though long since the man who lighted it, Alban Berg, has been taken away, suddenly, at the age of fifty, is a great and forever inspiring token for the magic power of the mind. For Berg, so famous a composer, so powerful a figure in the history of modern art, has written incredibly little: a piano sonata, two string quartets, a few songs, pieces for clarinet and piano, a chamber concerto, the violin concerto (written on a commission for the violinist Louis Krasner *To the Memory of an Angel*, Alma Maria Mahler's daughter who had died at an early age), Wozzeck, and parts of *Lulu*, his second opera, based on a book by Frank Wedekind but left unfinished. Of these works, only a few have made a permanent mark. The others have almost vanished. Yet the light shines bright, the name is inscribed forever, a lovely, sparkling star is set in the firmament.

It was my great fortune, a source of unforgettable happiness, that I could accompany Alban Berg, the great composer, the wonderful human being, through the ups and downs of the ten years that were still given to him. A few years after the spectacular opening of Wozzeck the small theater in Oldenburg performed the work. When they celebrated an anniversary of some sort a little later, they asked me, among others, for a testimonial. I wrote a letter, emphasizing the fact that they had been in the avant-garde of those who had believed in Alban Berg. "The name of the Oldenburg Theater will always be connected with the fate of one of the great operas of our time, *Wozzeck*," I wrote. I signed the letter with my name and title as director of Universal's opera department. A few months later I received a copy of the anniversary booklet, in which my letter had been published. It came from Alban Berg. After the words "will always be connected" he had inserted an asterisk in red pencil, and at the bottom of the page, before my printed name and rank, he had inserted just two words—*ebenso wie*, just as.

Among the trophies of my life, this is the proudest. As I look at it in its little black frame here on my wall, I know that not everything has been in vain.

Wozzeck, of course, was only one of many adventures of that flamboyant period, the "Periclean age of the European operatic stage." One year there would be a "Handel Renaissance," sweeping the chain of eighty and more subsidized opera houses: old scores were dusted off; designers, stage directors, technicians, musical wizards got busy; strange, abstract podiums would be erected, bathed in magic lights. Singers and dancers on stilts, in flowing robes, tried to bring back the forgotten heroes of Israel, Greece, and Rome. Most of these works were soon laid to rest again: the judgment of musical history is terrible but just, and exhumations of bodies, no matter how well preserved they appear, only rarely bring back the departed souls. But it didn't matter: the event itself, the enthusiasm, the spiritual exercise was reward enough. Nothing that happens in the realm of art is ever altogether lost.

Another year would see Darius Milhaud, composer, and Paul Claudel, ambassador-poet, get together to write a strange, symbolistic tale of Christopher Columbus. The fantastic technical apparatus and the unexhaustible resources of the Berlin Opera House welded together by the powerful energy of its musical leader, Erich Kleiber, gave the work a startling presentation. Or there would be a new opera by my friend Max Brand, bringing the mysteries of modern machines on the operatic stage—the moaning voices of turbines, roaring dynamos, sad cries of little cogwheels. What a time we had preparing the startling production in Duisburg on the Rhine, twenty-five stagehands working the groaning machines and eerie lights, a chorus backstage humming the music of the huge make-believe assembly line, and the only real thing in the fantastic irreality of the stage a blue-eyed Rhinemaiden, a member of the ballet, who was to make a short appearance towards the end of the opera and was bored almost beyond rescue, waiting for her cue in the lonely darkness of the wings. She had to be rescued from boredom in the interest of the production—and rescued she was. Thank you, Stadttheater Duisburg.

A new Schönberg, devilishly difficult and highly unsuccessful, made its bow after one hundred back-, heart-, budget-breaking rehearsals. In the little Bavarian town of

Koburg, I would meet Francesco Malipiero, who had come from his dream house in Asolo near Venice for a tryout of one of his operatic fantasies. In Frankfurt, of all places in the world, an audience was to see George Antheil's operatic transcription of an American presidential election. George and I were a minority of two who loved the work. Fabulous animals came to life in Leos Janáček's fabulous story of the *Sly Fox*. Paul Hindemith brought the rattling of typewriters onto the opera stage and added an aria, sung by a lady in a bathtub, to the *News of the Day*. Darius Milhaud wrote a series of *Opéras-Minutes*, concentrated versions of Greek tragedies, flying by in five to eight flimsy minutes. When a home-coming athlete was welcomed by a German official as the finest ambassador of good will the nation had known, Ernst Krenek had him on the stage of the Wiesbaden Opera House in no time—*Heavyweight* or *The Pride of the Nation* followed his sensational *Jonny Spielt Auf*, an opera that had glorified and at the same satirized the jazz age of the early twenties, had played on every stage of Europe, and made a fortune for its author.

What life there was, what enterprise, what spirit. There were one hundred failures for one success—no, two hundred, five hundred flops for one work of significance. It didn't matter. That is the way it should be. Failures are the fertilizer of artistic life. They are expendable. Thousands have to die so that a few may survive. There was *Wozzeck*. There was *Jenufa*. There was *Oedipus Rex*. There was *Dreigroschenoper*. There was *Matthis der*

Maler. Enough to justify a whole era. More than enough.

It wasn't success, measured in public recognition or in money, that made these years productive, unforgettable, unextinguishable years. It was the basic disregard for success in its established form, the perpetual struggle for new forms of expression, the daring and imagination of writers, composers, stage directors, dancers, conductors, even impresarios that gave these years such significance. Success came where it was not planned, not even expected, a sudden blessing out of the dark. Things done the easy way meant nothing. A new, expensive, lavishly endowed, and braggingly advertised production of *Don Carlo, Carmen, Aïda, Rigoletto*—with wonderful singers, brand-new sets, an orchestra of ninety-five, and a maestro of world-shaking importance in the pit—meant nothing, nothing at all. There were hundreds of them, there still are, in Berlin, in Milan, and in New York. They are here today, gone tomorrow. The expensive sets are painted over, the tenor puts on too much fat, the maestro makes room for a bigger maestro of strictly interspacial importance, the ambitious general manager is sent back to the showers. Who cares? It has not added anything to the substance of the time. It has not enriched the spiritual world. Soap bubbles—big, colorful. Puff. Gone.

But the memory of an evening in a shabby gymnasium in Baden-Baden back in 1927 is still alive. There were no stars on the little stage, no expensive scenery, no complicated machines. But who of those who were there will ever forget the first showing of Kurt Weill's *Mahagonny*

—and even if none of us will be around to remember the day, the work will still be here, the "mysterious magic," the "strange radiation of a spiritual deed."

Kurt Weill, my friend for many years, a man exactly my age—we were both born in 1900—is gone. His picture looks at me from the wall, next to the ethereal features of Béla Bartók, the beautiful, proud face of Alban Berg. There is no tragedy in Kurt's smiling, suspicious, very alert eyes behind the sparkling glasses, no sadness in the mocking lips, casually holding a dangling pipe, in the bald forehead, the elegant, expensive-looking suit, the signature of a famous commercial photographer at the bottom of the picture. His was a full, a determined, a successful life. When I think of him I think of his dry humor, his relentless self-criticism, his sarcasm, his clever, penetrating mind. How I miss his phone calls, the visits in his lovely house by the brook in New City in Rockland County, the good talks, the festive meals, the planning for a future that never came. . . .

The appearance of *Mahagonny* at the music festival in Baden-Baden, in the summer of 1927, had been a tremendous shock. It was just a string of little choruses and songs, the music a skillful blending of jazz and blues rhythms heard and projected most originally through a very European mind—a surrealistic reflection of jazz and blues. Marching songs and simple folksy tunes were carried by a little orchestra full of sobbing saxophones and schmalzy fiddles. And all this was played against the background of a festival devoted to atonal cello sonatas and settings of Petrarchian sonnets for string trio, voice, and solo oboe. Most of the assembled musicians were shocked beyond belief. The public in the audience, who didn't know that they weren't supposed to, clapped and shouted their approval. Some left the hall happily humming the tunes. Nothing like it had ever marred a modern music festival. It was a terrible disappointment. What had happened to Kurt Weill?

He had grown up in a very different musical atmosphere and had been expected to be "one of the boys." Neither the frivolous tunes of *Mahagonny* nor a house in Rockland County with a private brook nor the $300,000 paid by Hollywood for the film rights in Kurt Weill's *Lady in the Dark*—the highest fee yet paid for a Broadway musical—seemed visible in the crystal ball when Kurt Weill left his native Dessau (where he was born the son of a Jewish cantor) and set out for near-by Berlin to cement the education which had begun in the musical atmosphere of his parental home.

At night he played the piano in a *Bierkeller*—but the days were spent in very different surroundings. Weill had become a pupil of Ferruccio Busoni, high-minded and austere theoretician of music, composer of serious concertos and slightly anemic operas. Clad in silk and velvet, the master would compose during the morning in an inner sanctum that nobody was allowed to enter. At lunch time he emerged, consumed half a bottle of French champagne, and then presided over a table that always attracted a number of admiring guests. Solemn were the conversations, golden the words.

After coffee had been served by a silent butler, the guests, aware of the ritual of the house, took their leave. The pupils arrived. There are no echoes of the nocturnal *Bierkeller* in the string quartets, orchestral scores, the cycle of songs to early German poems which Kurt Weill wrote in the velvety, silken atmosphere of his teacher.

But soon there were signs of defection. In 1924, when he was twenty-four, Weill came across a one-act play *The Protagonist*, by Georg Kaiser, best described as the German O'Neill of the period. It was a play about an actor who tragically confuses stage and life and commits a real murder while acting. The young composer wrote to the famous playwright, obtained an interview, and got permission to set *The Protagonist* to music. At its successful première in Dresden, Oscar Bie, one of Germany's leading critics, praised the blending of music and drama and pointed out the irony of this success of a youthful pupil of Busoni in his first attempt in the operatic field, a field where success had consistently eluded the master himself. "All the philosophical theories of teacher Busoni have been swept aside by the reality of Kurt Weill's score," Bie wrote.

And now *Mahagonny!* This time the words were by Bert Brecht, the great, utterly unrefined German poet, a master with words, full of uninhibited originality and an earthy power, detrimental in every idea, every thought, every ribald joke to the olympian world of Busoni. Ma-

hagonny was a make-believe town in a make-believe
America that neither Weill nor his libretto writer had
ever seen. Some of the words were written in a make-
believe English, a basic international Americanese. Lotte
Lenja, Kurt's wife, led the chorus with a husky, haunting
voice, floating across the primitive stage with edgy, quite
unreal, deeply moving gestures, singing, speaking, dancing
the broad melodies and the lilting rhythm, the deep sadness and the beautiful resignation of the music:

> "Oh moon of Alabama
>   We now must say good-by
> We've lost our good old mama
>   And must have whiskey, oh you know why . . ."

It was clear, simple, beautiful. Compared with it, the wild
antics of The Protagonist were pure high-brow. "I am
not struggling for new forms or new theories," Weill now
declared. "I am struggling for a new public."

Soon the struggle was carried even further. Brecht and
Weill wrote a school opera—the first time, probably, that
writers of professional standing had attempted anything
of the kind. Their singers and musicians were to be the
purest of all amateurs: children. The work was called Der
Jasager—the Boy Who Says Yes. It was a hard, a cruel
story, based on an old Japanese play: the story of a boy
who consents to sacrifice his life so that others may succeed in an important mission. I have staged the little
work with school children in one of Vienna's poorest dis-
tricts. Never have I seen an audience so deeply moved as

by the simple lines and primitive melodies of this score. As I am writing these lines, so many years later and with an ocean, a war, an era between myself and that group of youngsters, I can still see the solemn procession of small children walking away from the little hero, praising his sacrifice with sad pride. I can still hear the music, the little voice, trembling with excitement, the sob of a mother in the audience, the violent storm of applause, more genuine and deep than the applause that curls at the feet of the great and in the condescending nostrils of the exalted.

Then, in the summer of 1928, Brecht and Weill applied their theories to a new version of the *Beggar's Opera*, the famous *Dreigroschenoper*. Brecht rewrote the two-hundred-year-old play to make it a brilliant and gripping discourse on the evils and dangers of our time. Weill wrote a new score. The work became, at once, a tremendous success.

Just a little while ago I heard some of the music again. It was at a memorial to Kurt Weill in Town Hall, New York. In the twenty-two years that had elapsed since *Dreigroschenoper*, he had become a successful, recognized, rich man in America. *The Eternal Road, Johnny Jonson, Knickerbocker Holiday, Lady in the Dark, One Touch of Venus, Street Scene, Down in the Valley, Lost in the Stars*, and after Georg Kaiser and Bert Brecht an incredible array of famous writers who had yielded to the Kurt Weill spell and his infallible grip for the stage: Franz Werfel, Paul Green, Maxwell Anderson, Moss

Hart, Elmer Rice, Langston Hughes, Arnold Sundgard. There had been one composer who had never been plagued by the eternal curse that even Mozart, Verdi, and Strauss could not always resolve—the lack of a libretto. Playwrights, ordinarily distrustful of the ivory-tower composer, found themselves confronted by a man who knew just as much if not more than they did about the laws of the theater. To the very last day of his life Kurt Weill had been a success—up to the very last hour he had worked and planned with his friend and neighbor Maxwell Anderson on still another promising Broadway production, a dramatization of *Huckleberry Finn*.

But we were not thinking of all this as we were sitting in Town Hall to pay our last respects to our departed friend. Lotte Lenja was again on stage, singing and acting and looking as if time had stood still. We all sat there, listening to the husky, soft voice, watching those edgy, unreal, deeply moving gestures, trembling in our seats, unable to hold back the tears as the old wonderful songs swept through the hall, full of meaning and memories. The rousing song of the soldiers that live on the cannons. The *Ballad of Macky Messer*. Jenny's soft, catlike voice telling of the ship with ten sails and with forty guns, coming into the harbor, silent, at night, while the town is asleep. It unloads its terrible cargo: pirates, Jenny's, Pirate-Jenny's friends, ready to kill anyone in the town she wants to have killed. Jenny standing by the pier and watching the poor wretches brought in and smiling quietly and saying "Hoop-la!" as each head rolls.

The music and the words had lost nothing of their power and significance, nothing of the brilliant strength of a great creative period that was gone, dead, buried beyond resurrection and yet alive in its works of the spirit. Soon after the words had been written and the music had been played, we all stood at the pier, watching in horror as the ships came in and the pirates, merciless, swept the land. Even Jenny didn't smile any more.

> "Oh moon of Alabama
> We now must say good-by
> We've lost our good old mama . . ."

It was no opera any more. It was stark, bloody, terrible truth.

We had lost our good old mama.

It was time to say good-by.

Reunion

The new mama wasn't very kind at first.

An opera maniac in America! Steven Strode, the commuting Croesus, was not the only one who looked at me with indignation at the thought that he should give up a pinochle game on the 5.47 for an after-dinner auto-da-fé on the stage of the Metropolitan Opera House. It seemed a commonly accepted fact, never doubted and scarcely questioned, that this country wasn't giving a hoot about opera. Opera was an Un-American Activity: foreign singers, conductors, and managers, presenting foreign works in foreign language to a selected audience which paid outrageous prices for the privilege to arrive before the first intermission and to leave as soon as the lights were dimmed for the last act.

Once a year, in New York, San Francisco, New Orleans, and in some of the cities where the Met stopped on its whirlwind tours of "the provinces," the newspapers carried pictures of ermine-caped ladies and top-hatted gents, descending from broad limousines, ascending broad stairways, dining and wining at intermission time, occasionally putting an ancient leg on a marble table as a fitting symbol for the hilarity of the occasion. Tales of terrible catastrophes went around: the Insull debacle that had left nothing behind but the taste-less sausage of a misshaped opera house in Chicago. The collapse of a more recent but not less disastrous venture in Philadelphia. The plight of singers who had no place to go. The Metropolitan's regularly recurrent troubles and public appeals for alms—a state of affairs that had once been hurled so triumphantly at my sensitive, freshly imported European ears in Steven Strode's unforgettable summation: "If they don't make money, why don't they close the joint."

Opera, the consensus was, unless prefixed by "horse" or "soap," will never catch on in America. Forget it.

Even the creative musicians seemed to share the gen-eral feeling of hopelessness. Most American composers shied away from opera, devoting their time to the accu-mulation of a tremendous repertoire of symphonies, con-certos, and chamber music. If they entered the theater at all, they did so through the back door, writing ballet scores for Martha Graham or Agnes de Mille in the seclu-sion of their studios, far removed from the hot breath and thumping life of the stage. No one was more surprised than the composers themselves when they saw what the good ladies did to their scores. The stage life of the music was short. It soon left the incestuous bed of the theater to appear as a strait-laced suite or long-skirted tone poem on the concert stage, where it was much happier and perfectly at home.

It all didn't make sense. One had only to walk over to Broadway to see the teeming wealth of dramatic talent in America: great, constructive activity in every department of the theater. When I returned to Europe for my first visit after the war I felt its radiations everywhere: in Brussels it was *Un tramway nommé désir*; in Vienna *Der Tod des Handelsreisenden*; in Zürich *Unsere kleine Stadt*; in Rotterdam something that sounded like an advertisement for Liederkranz and turned out to be *The Iceman Cometh*. American ballet companies and symphony orchestras were all over the place.

Why should opera be the Cinderella, never to be admitted to the great American ball? Why should the public in Chemnitz, Graz, Berne, or Copenhagen be more musical, more opera-minded than the public in Cleveland, St. Louis, Oakland, or Kalamazoo? It could be a question of economics. Or maybe it was just a question of time. Things had started late in America. When everything was already organized, musically, in Europe, the continent literally dotted with symphony orchestras and opera houses, they had just begun to clear the roads through the American wilderness.

But the sudden and rapid growth of American musical culture, so long retarded and so belatedly begun, has pro-

duced many strange and revolutionary patterns. Never
before and nowhere else had one hundred and fifty symphony orchestras been created and firmly established
within the short period of one human generation. Never
before had prospectors traversed a tremendous continent
to organize, overnight, musical chain stores in two thousand communities. Almost two hundred centers of musical learning were created between the two World Wars.
Such seemingly age-old, full-bearded, and already a little
arthritic institutions as the Curtis, Juilliard, and Eastman
schools of music, the Cleveland, Los Angeles, or Washington, D.C., symphony, the New Friends of Music,
Ravinia Park, or the NBC Symphony were founded only
in our own time.

They, and hundreds of others, are the descendants of
the radio age. It was radio that brought the message of
music for the first time into millions of American homes.
Toscanini, not a fifth-rate *Stadttheaterkapellmeister*, was
the first to conduct an orchestral concert for hundreds of
American communities. The Metropolitan Opera's star-
studded shows, broadcast elaborately every Saturday afternoon, were their first contact with grand opera. They
heard Artur Rubinstein, Lotte Lehmann, the Boston
Symphony before they began to organize their own local
places of musical worship. The radio age made them
music-conscious, inspired them to organize their own
symphony orchestras, to add music departments to their
universities, to make their children play in bands, to hire
full-time music teachers for their high schools, to buy

classical records, to import string quartets, to attend community concerts.

During its short reign, radio effected a complete transformation of the American musical scene. Elsewhere in the world it had only been a new way of communication. Here it created entirely new conditions, a spiritual atmosphere that had not existed at all before. It condensed three centuries of European musical history into thirty action-packed American years.

And now Television has arrived. Radio is rapidly giving up its musical ambitions. Again a vast, radical transformation is in the making as the eye as well as the ear becomes engaged. Again it is not only an added medium of communication but a means of creating new musical, cultural conditions, entirely unknown to the country in the past. A new interest in the *visible* side of music is already plainly evident.

Its first startling signs appeared when ballets began to catch the imagination of the American public. Ballets are sissy, ballets are stupid, a ballet, unless presented by heel-clicking Rockettes or cancanning Ziegfeld girls, will never catch on in America. Forget it. Wasn't that another one of those basic rules which all the Steven Strodes of the continent have laid down? But now it isn't only sophisticated New York that jams every performance of the Ballet Theatre, the Sadler's Wells, the City Center Ballet, the ballets from Paris, Madrid, or Monte Carlo. The citizens of St. Louis, Cleveland, Oakland, and Kalamazoo are just as susceptible to beauty, great music, grace, artistic perfection, and artistic integrity as are the people anywhere else in the world. They like the *Skaters Waltz*—who doesn't—but they also crowd the ballets of Schönberg and Stravinsky and are touched by the brilliant, uncompromising presentations of the finest choreographers of two continents. The best and the finest is recognized and is just good enough for them.

Is it an accident that this happens at the dawn of the television age? A new chapter in the unorthodox history of music in America is about to begin. Is it too fanciful a conclusion that the acceptance of ballet is only a beginning, that television will do for opera in America what radio has done for symphonic music? From where I sit it is no paper dream. Miss Bishop, walking in with the afternoon mail, is the lovely harbinger of wonderful and miraculous tidings. Opera, opera, opera—letters, not from Vienna this time, not from Duisburg and Milan, but from Bloomington, Los Angeles, Baton Rouge, Des Moines, Tulsa, Salt Lake City, Minneapolis, Miami Beach. After years of celibacy, I have found my ladylove again. She has changed a little. She has lost some of her turbulent gowns. A few stones are missing from her tiara. The giants in her train are a little smaller and the dwarfs not quite so small. It doesn't matter. What happens to me as I glance over these letters and talk to the people and go out in the field to see what they are doing is again what happened in the days of *Mahagonny*, of *Jonny Spielt Auf*, of *Der Jasager*, of *Wozzeck*. Again it is new, unorthodox, experimental. Again it is just a beginning and nobody knows where it will end. It is a wonderful, miraculous, and never-hoped-for recurrence of a former life.

With all its fame and splendor, the Metropolitan Opera House, the very essence of operatic life in America, is not part of the new venture yet. The Met is changing slowly. The voice of its intermission announcer loses a little bit of its pompous exaltation when he describes the splendor of Miss Nikolaides' costume to an awed audience in Upper Montclair. In its repertory, its style of productions, its public relations, it is trying to loosen up. It has formed a second company that plays in movie houses and high-school auditoriums. It is slowly turning its wrinkled, snobbish face towards the fresh breezes that stroke the fields of the land. But it is no accident that its building—now almost smothered between the ugliest skyscrapers that ever peeked in at a performance of *Die Meistersinger*—is located closer to New York Harbor than any other center of American spiritual life. Through the music that fills its sedate auditorium blow the whistles of the boats that come in from Italy, France, and Germany, and you can attend a performance as a spectator, a singer, a general manager and still easily catch the *Queen Mary*, sailing at midnight for points east. Bon Voyage.

But a few blocks further inland the atmosphere changes rapidly. At the Juilliard School, uptown, near Riverside Church, one can see intensely designed and strikingly presented performances of new works: Dallapiccola's *Prisoner*, for instance, or the Benjamin Britten version of the *Beggar's Opera*, Stravinsky's *Oedipus Rex*, a gripping masterpiece grippingly hammered into grateful ears, or his *Soldier's Tale*, with Dimitri Mitropoulos coming uptown from his job as the conductor of the New York Philharmonic Orchestra to direct the show and to act himself on the stage.

The Mannes School presents delightful shows at the charming Hunter Playhouse. What chuckling delight among an enthusiastic audience when their singers and dancers marched through the little auditorium, introducing to America, in a triumphant procession, Martinu's opera, *Comedy on the Bridge*. The City Center now has two big seasons of opera in the fall and spring of each year. A rich repertory of brand-new works and old war horses, popularly priced, popularly presented, is a riotous, popular success.

At Columbia University a genuine operatic tradition has been established. Benjamin Britten, the wonder boy, had his first operatic attempt performed on the stage of the Brander Matthews Theatre on 118th Street: his soaringly unsuccessful setting of W. W. Auden's version of *Paul Bunyan*. Virgil Thomson's *Mother of Us All*, to a libretto by Gertrude Stein, was presented on the little stage. Virgil T. and Gertrude S. sang prettily, old hymn tunes and barn dances startled the listeners, and while it may not have been a success in the commonly accepted, worn-out sense of the word, it has not been forgotten. It still lives in the mind of man, pops up again and again in conversation. It has added to the spiritual substance of the time. That is success, real and important, weightier than the successes measurable in royalty checks, in interviews on Pier 90, in the headlines of today that are only fuel for tomorrow's barbecue.

And now my ladylove, having guided her bacchantian cortège all over town—to Broadway even, to the Edison Hotel for performances "in the round," to a church basement in Greenwich Village—has led her inspiring parade into the solemn environs of Carnegie Hall. What could be a clearer indication of the deep change in the musical fortunes of the land than the successfully sustained invasion of the American concert stage by opera. Gone are the days when Melchior was standing up there, white-tied and black-tailed, to announce to the uneasy subscribers that *Winterstürme wichen dem Wonnemond*. In Town Hall, Thomas Scherman and his Little Orchestra have given a whole series of Mozart operas in superb renditions, among them *Idomeneo*, never before heard in New York. Mitropoulos has made opera a regular feature of his Philharmonic programs, and all over the nation the new trend is unmistakable. Complete performances of *Carmen*, *Pagliacci*, of Verdi's *Othello*, Strauss's *Elektra* or *Salome*, of dozens of other operas, presented with singers, chorus, and orchestra, have become featured events of almost every symphony orchestra in the nation. The conductors who select them, the management who pays for them know that the public, suddenly aroused to the unique beauty of opera, will be attracted by them

more surely than by the customary concert soloist, no
matter how dazzling the name or how famous the concerto.

It is a new, creative solution of problems typical of the
American scene today. There are no Stadttheaters, no
subsidies, few facilities to produce opera in the grand
style outside of a few privileged centers. What, then,
could be more logical, more constructive, than to make
the best of what there is: to combine the local resources—
symphony orchestras, university choruses, singers—and to
produce opera with the maximum musical fidelity and
with as much stage illusion as can be provided? It is a
strong, stimulating beginning—not perfect, not by a long
shot, but better, I should think, than sitting by, bemoan-
ing the shortcomings of this country in the field of opera
and nursing sickly memories of wonderful operatic seasons in Wuppertal. Most of the opera performances in
Wuppertal, friend, look and sound wonderful only in our
memories. While we were sitting there, you and I, looking at them and listening to the town band playing in the
pit and the miserable crew of singers yodeling on stage,
we knew they stank.

There is a new style emerging for these semi-operatic
American presentations of operas. The formal limitations
of the concert stage are loosened up just enough and not
too much. "Basic costumes" are being introduced, "basic
sets," "basic gestures"—a new fascinating challenge to
conductors and stage directors, a new fascination to audiences, a new chance for singers. The results can be strik-

ing—in many cases more so than the cheap make-believe world of musty scenery, talmi costumes, hammy gestures that are the arsenal of many "real" operatic performances throughout the world. Who will ever forget Mitropoulos' performance of *Wozzeck* in Carnegie Hall? It will set a pattern for a long time to come.

The first stroke of excitement touched the audience before the music began. Some of the singers, entering with the conductor as they would for any oratorio and taking their seats in front of the audience, were in shirt sleeves. The women wore cheap dresses, the doctor and the captain formal, slightly old-fashioned cutaways. That was all the costuming there was—but just to see these artists, where one usually saw bassos in immaculate white vests and sopranos in glittering silver lamé, created a nervous atmosphere of expectation. The magic wand of opera had touched the hall before the imaginary curtain went up.

The acting was just as "basic"—restrained, yet overwhelmingly clear. A few steps, a turning of the head, a raising of the hand, a sadistic grin, a stare of deep, deep despair. A chair or two, a platform in the rear. But when a man suddenly jumped on a chair while delivering a drunken speech to the startled members of the Schola Cantorum, Carnegie Hall, without the benefit of scenery or light effects, was transformed into a German beer garden. Mr. Frederick Jagel, the tenor, was sitting all the time in his chair, waiting for his cue. When he got up, swaying slightly from too much *Branntewein*, the small-sized singer was suddenly the big, bragging lover, the *Tambourmajor* who, for all time, will outshout, outdrink, outlove all the poor Wozzecks in the world. Everybody saw him enter—not just another section of the Carnegie Hall podium—but a small, smelly room in a German barracks where Mr. Hugh Ross, the dignified director of the Schola singers, sitting in the rear among his dignified members, was magically transformed into a poor, starving soldier, dreaming uneasily among humming, uneasy dreamers.

While Wozzeck was drowning, the doctor and the captain appeared on a platform in the rear of the stage. Wozzeck—Mr. Mack Harrell, that is—was still sitting in his chair, next to the conductor, plainly visible to anyone in the audience who still was able to see him. Yet there was no doubt that he was drowning, pitifully, and quite beyond rescue, and when the doctor, attired in modern clothes, on a primitive platform above the viola section, exclaimed, *"Da stirbt ein Mensch,"* Wozzeck died a more horrible and more definite death than if he had walked off the stage of an opera house into the rescuing arms of assistant stage manager Hopfenbacher.

Significant as all these new departures are, and indicative of a new approach towards the problems of the musical theater in America, they are only a small segment of a much broader picture. A survey on operatic activities in the United States, taking into account only groups that performed complete operatic works, shows more than two hundred organizations actively engaged in the production of operas. This is a hell of a lot of opera—even if measured by European yardsticks. Who are the people, the groups, the organizations who have sprung up, quite suddenly, all over the land and have commenced a serious and far-reaching attempt to establish opera in the United States?

First, to be sure, there is the small number of professional companies, presenting traditional opera in traditional style: the Metropolitan, which appears in New York and some twenty other cities and which recently added a second road company, one that tours while the main body of the establishment is busy in New York—the Little Met, so to say. It actually amounts to two Mets being in operation simultaneously. It means employment for many more singers, enjoyment for many more people. It's still another straw in a mighty, relentless wind.

The San Francisco Opera has a six-week season of standard fare, a pre-Metropolitan season of the West, drawing almost exclusively from the roster of the Metropolitan artists and conductors and closing as soon as everybody has to depart for the opening of the Met. New Orleans carries on one of the oldest American traditions of opera in a highly formal social setting. The New York City Opera has become a springboard for new works and new voices. There are a few additional professional groups: the Charles L. Wagner company, giving one-night stands in 119 different cities, the Cincinnati Summer Zoo Opera, the Connecticut Opera Association in

Hartford, and an occasional *stagione* such as the San
Carlo, Salmaggi, or Philadelphia La Scala.

But these are not the names that call from the papers
on my desk. New names make themselves heard, strange
and far-off places, dozens and dozens of "opera producers" of a very different caliber. In Pittsburgh the
College of Fine Arts at Carnegie Institute of Technology
presents "for the first time in its history" an opera—an
arena-style production of Mozart's *Marriage of Figaro*—
the Pennsylvania College for Women announces a series
of performances of a contemporary American work, and
still another group presents a series of standard operas.
The Lyric Theater of Karamu House in Cleveland reports
fifty performances of a new opera by Carl Orff, more
than one hundred performances of Kurt Weill's *Lost in
the Stars*, productions of Stravinsky's *Histoire du Soldat*,
Gluck's *Caravan to Mecca*, and similar unconventional
presentations. All the participants are local people, most
of them amateurs. One of them, a Cleveland housewife
making her first stage appearance as Baba in Karamu's
production of *The Medium*, made such an impression
that she was brought to New York in the same part. Now
the Play House, Cleveland's progressive dramatic theater,
likewise announces the addition of operatic works to its
repertory.

In Greenville, South Carolina, Bob Jones University
presents Verdi's *Ernani* and other ambitious operatic
works. In the same town Furman University announces
that the departments of music and speech are combining

forces in a new opera workshop. In Seattle a Swedish count, Mikael Scheremetiew, organizes a group that during its first season gave, among other works, the Northwest premières of Tchaikovsky's *Eugene Onegin* and Gershwin's *Porgy and Bess*. In Seattle, too, the music department of the University of Washington is actively engaged in the production of operas, concentrating particularly on contemporary works.

San Antonio, one of the eleven towns in Texas that now have permanent symphony orchestras (there was not a single one in the state fifteen years ago), puts on an annual festival of four operas. Six thousand people, many of them traveling two hundred and fifty miles and more, see performances of *Tristan*, *Figaro*, *Rosenkavalier*, and *The Old Maid and the Thief*. Now the symphony orchestra of Kansas City will do the same: an annual festival of opera, combining the local forces of the orchestra, the chorus, the conductor Hans Schwieger, with experienced singers, imported from New York.

In Los Angeles, the City College Opera Studio gives regular performances of chamber operas, old and new, while at the University of Southern California, Carl Ebert, my old friend of pre-Hitler operatic battles in Darmstadt and Berlin, puts on *Ariadne on Naxos*, Menotti's *The Consul*, or the world première of a new opera by Ernst Krenek. Ebert, professor at the University of Southern California (from where he goes regularly to stage operas at the Scala in Milan, at Glyndbourne, Edinburgh, and Venice), runs the university's opera department on a highly professional level; most of his singers are already actively working in the field and return to the university to receive advanced training and to participate in Ebert's productions. He is also head of the Los Angeles Guild Opera, probably the first American group to receive an outright subsidy from a public agency: $25,000 per year from Los Angeles County. With this group (which also gives employment to as many of his university students as possible) Ebert gives performances of such works as *Il Seraglio, The Bartered Bride,* and *Hansel and Gretel* (which he performed several times for audiences of six thousand school children at the Shrine Auditorium) in Hollywood, Los Angeles, and Pasadena. The University of Minnesota Opera Theatre gave a series of performances of Menotti's *The Medium* with such encouraging reaction from the students and the authorities of the university that it is now a permanent institution and one of the most popular departments of the university. In Spartanburg, South Carolina, a Lyric Opera Company, under the guidance of the faculty of the School of Music of Converse College, "makes articulate the natural gifts of many of the townspeople and serves as a testing place for new American works and for singers who need experience." In Des Moines, Iowa . . .

But the list could be continued almost indefinitely.

Even more amazing than the scope of all these enterprises is the fact that they sprang up virtually overnight and with sweeping simultaneity. Most of them have been operating only a few years—many just for two or three seasons. Almost none of them was in existence prior to World War II. As far back as 1931 the Juilliard School began to commission and produce new operas and to create some sort of independent, progressive operatic unit. It commissioned and performed Louis Gruenberg's *Jack and the Beanstalk*, adding works by George Antheil (*Helen Retires*, 1934), Robert Russell Bennett (*Maria Malibran*, 1935), Albert Stoessel (*Garrick*, 1937), and Beryl Rubinstein (*The Sleeping Beauty*, 1938). In 1934, Virgil Thomson's first opera, *Four Saints in Three Acts*, was produced by the Society of Friends and Enemies of Modern Music in Hartford, Connecticut, after six years had elapsed since the completion of the score. Aaron Copland's only operatic work so far, the high-school opera *The Second Hurricane*, was first given by the children of the Henry Street Music School in New York in 1937.

All this occurred in a vacuum. It was of no immediate consequence. To the country at large, outside of New York and a few similar centers, it meant little. No operatic facilities, no interest, no willingness to carry through were in evidence. Even the now famous Opera Workshop of Columbia University in New York began its activities only as recently as 1941.

The spirit behind such a sudden, in its forcefulness and universality unprecedented development, its cultural significance, its intentions, and its ultimate goal are simple and identical all over the country. But it has many new ways of manifestation. There is no general formula. It is done differently in different places. In Europe it is and has been a simple matter. The state gives you an opera house, an orchestra, and all the money you need. Go ahead and produce opera, ten months a year. Here there isn't any such thing. So how is it done? How do the people go about it? What makes it tick?

This desk of mine is a wonderful place for research. No books, no musty librarians, no waiting till the man comes in with a mountain of clippings so that I can extract a little mouse of wisdom. All I have to do is press a button. In floats Miss Bishop, her lovely arms loaded with folders. I take one, any one, open it, and there is a story!

Miss Bishop's Folders

Portland, says the first folder, Portland, Oregon, and "thanks for giving us the green light on Menotti's *The Consul*," it says. "We will produce the opera in a theater seating close to one thousand. You might be a little surprised that we can give such a production here—complete with orchestra, scenery, singers. Well, we are surprised ourselves. Let me tell you how it all started.

"In the summer of 1949 I had prepared a group of singers and an amateur orchestra in Debussy's *L'Enfant Prodigue*. Then I recalled that there is, in one of our city parks, a beautiful, natural amphitheater with box hedges for wings and backstage; it had never been used before for any type of theatrical production. We asked the city for permission to use it for a Saturday and a Sunday afternoon show, free to the public. On the first day we had about a thousand people—

but the next afternoon they had mysteriously multiplied
—four thousand had come to hear Debussy! The city was
delighted by this novel use of its park and offered what
help they could give for the future.

"The next year, with the aid of facilities of the Park
Bureau of the city (set construction, moving of musical
instruments, et cetera), and with dancers trained and
provided by them, we embarked upon the production of
Aïda. The Musicians Union extended their co-operation
this time by permitting union musicians to play without
recompense, a mixed blessing as it made for a 'now you
see it, now you don't' orchestra from rehearsal to rehearsal. We gave two performances of Aïda, free to the
public, to an estimated eleven thousand people. To cover
our expenses we sold advertising space in our programs.

"The following winter the city decided to hold a festival in conjunction with the city's one hundredth anniversary. In addition to the opera, there was a Park Bureau
ballet production of Midsummer Night's Dream, band
concerts, a chamber orchestra concert, square and folk
dancing. The festival took place over a period of twelve
days, three of which were occupied by our production of
Carmen. The city's help was greatly amplified. Again they
provided set construction, instrument moving. In addition, they set up a fine lighting and sound system and
took over the problem of orchestral musicians for the
opera by operating concessions for coke, coffee, and pop-
corn, the proceeds of which went directly to the musicians. We had an adequate orchestra without expense

and a group of pleased musicians. Twenty-one thousand were present at the three performances of *Carmen!*"

Twenty-one thousand people seeing a local production of *Carmen* in Portland, Oregon—that's news, Miss Bishop. We'll let them do *The Consul* for half the usual fee. We are building up customers. It used to be Wuppertal, now it is Portland. What is next?

Next is Miss Charlotte Louise Shockley, in private life a librarian, and, by vocation, a singer, publicity director, and general manager of the Cincinnati Music Drama Guild. The Guild was founded in 1947 "to provide good entertainment and to encourage local artists in Cincinnati." It gives three or four productions every year— modern works by Britten, Weill, Menotti, Vaughan Williams, Douglas Moore, and classics—*Figaro*, for instance, *Barber of Seville, Hansel and Gretel,* and some special gems such as Puccini's *Tabarro* or Ravel's *L'Heure Espagnole.* Over two hundred Guild Workers are busy within its rapidly expanding frame. Except for the union musicians, nobody gets paid. "Hence," Miss Shockley comments, "no one resents any possible inequality. We all work and play together and have a wonderful time painting scenery, building sets, and learning roles. The city lets us use the Public Recreation Building, where we can rehearse and prepare our scenery to our hearts' content or sew costumes while we sing chorus."

Sounds pretty—sew costumes while they sing chorus in Cincinnati. I love the sound of it.

To get the season under way, while they are waiting for

the subscription money to come in (Miss Shockley, carried by the exuberance of her self-chosen mission, uses the word "pour in"—you see the mailmen staggering under their load), the Guild asks "philanthropic persons and business firms" for contributions. "However," Miss Shockley proclaims cheerfully, "we never get more than five or six hundred from that source, so we really operate on a shoestring. That's, of course, half of the fun. Here is one of our shoestring budgets. It tells you more than any letter could do on how the Cincinnati Stadttheater operates."

I adore figures. Who doesn't may turn to the next page, where he will find some lucid observations on the status of opera in English which I have been dying to put on paper for many years. But first:

THE CINCINNATI MUSIC DRAMA GUILD

FINANCIAL REPORT

PRODUCTION: KURT WEILL'S STREET SCENE

INCOME: Contributions (1/5) $ 160.38

         Ticket Sales

             Paid $1224.13

             Due   145.63   1369.76

Subscriptions   439.50

Programs   99.66

Refreshments & Checkroom—$45.85

     Coca-Cola $20.04

     Seven-Up   9.90   29.94   15.91

                             Total $2085.21

Less: Reserve for Federal Excise Tax*   308.33

                    Net Income $1776.88

PRODUCTION EXPENSES:

Salaries—Orchestra	$214.12
Salaries—Janitor	25.00
Accompanists' Fees	118.25
Salaries—Others	8.00
Royalty Fee	200.00
Musical Instrument Rental	75.90
Hall Rental	60.00
Costume Expenditures	33.29
Scenery Expenditures	40.56
Stage Properties	8.00
Décor Equipment	3.50
Miscellaneous Expenses	37.94
Make-Up	8.51
Lighting Equipment	36.01
Miscellaneous Promotion Expenses	55.48
Music Purchases	105.07
Advertising	75.12
Mailing Pieces and Cards	72.60
Posters	69.53
Photographs	68.00
Program Expense	58.84
Ticket Printing	11.95
Total Expenses	$1385.67
Net Profit (used for a scholarship)	$ 391.21

* This has now been eliminated, but even this small example shows the great importance and stimulating significance of the repeal of the strangulating Federal Tax on enterprises such as these!

It is no accident that the Cincinnati Music Drama Guild headlines all their publicity with the slogan *Operation English.* As the names of the Carmens and Figaros, the Mimis and Eisensteins become American names, their voices American voices, their language the language of Cincinnati, Spokane, and New York, the hotly tossed around question whether opera in America should be given in English becomes purely academic and utterly senseless. There can be only one final and definitive answer: Yes. It should, it has to, and it will.

To train American singers to parrot foreign sounds so that they can sing opera to American audiences in a language neither they nor their public understand is the acme of madness. And, please, do not say it is more "cultured" to sing a work in the language of the composer. To begin with, neither Mozart nor Verdi, Puccini nor Strauss, nor any other composer—including such living witnesses as Menotti, Britten, and Stravinsky—ever objected to their operas being sung in the language of the countries where they were performed. Quite to the contrary. The European countries, generally considered the cradle of opera and the centers of operatic life for centuries, have never subscribed to such abstruse theories.

In America, formerly, there were reasons for a different attitude—practical reasons, not wishy-washy theories. The singers that came here from foreign shores, the Carusos, the Chaliapins, the Schorrs, the Lehmanns not only were unable, of course, to sing their parts in English, but they also gave magnificent renderings of their roles in their native language, in their mother tongue which wasn't only the tongue of the composer but their own. Around them and their great performances a pious legend has been built—still proclaimed now under entirely different circumstances—that opera has to be produced in the composer's own tongue. That wasn't the point at all: Caruso didn't sing Rodolfo only in Puccini's language, but in his own. He was thinking, dreaming, loving, living, and dying in Italian, and when he sang in his own language he filled every word with a full measure of hidden meaning that made it vibrate with passion, beauty, color, with the century-old music of his blood.

But if Beethoven up there on his window ledge could have heard Miss Nadine Conner, a charming native of Compton, California, sing the part of Marcelline in *Fidelio* in what the program professed to be a German performance at the Metropolitan Opera House, he would have lost all his golden coating. Not only was the poor lady visibly handicapped by singing words she didn't understand—maybe she understood the words, but she did not feel the meaning behind them, never projected the hidden intensity, never made us hear what Lotte Lehmann, great and supreme master of the art of words, of background meanings, of secreted beauty, called More Than Singing—what was more: the sounds Miss Conner produced were not at all the sounds Beethoven had set to music. The whole theory that opera should be sung in the language of the composer was exposed in its supreme fallacy: Miss Conner sang the words but could never produce the sounds of Beethoven's German. One had only to listen to a few of the native German singers in the cast to realize the striking difference.

This thing has gone too far. In any Town Hall recital you can hear misled American youngsters torment themselves and their listeners with programs sung in four, five, and six different languages. I don't claim to be a judge of Italian, Spanish, or French, and my knowledge of Russian is limited to the tasty offerings of the Russian Tea Room. But I know German. And if the French, the Spanish, the Italian, and the Russian these poor kids had to learn (instead of using all that wasted time to penetrate the spirit of the music, which got completely lost in their frantic efforts to remember the proper Russian word for huckleberries), if their *français* and *espagnol* is as mistreated, forced, painfully parroted, and as far remote from the sounds Debussy, Fauré and De Falla set to music as is their German, something is very wrong.

It all comes out, quite clearly, when they finally reach the English group on their programs. Suddenly there is relaxation on their faces, the frozen smiles begin to thaw, their hearts are beating freely, the strait jacket is removed, the parrot is a nightingale again. A lover is something to kiss, not something to eat, and a flower not a succession of dreaded vowels and umlauts in bar 57 but something sweet, lovely, floating on the wings of music, enchanting the singer, the audience, the ushers, and even the critic of the *Herald Tribune*.

If these are the tribulations imposed by a few songs— what are the mental handicaps, the artistic restrictions on the operatic stage! Here, where life in its full three dimensions has to be portrayed, where it is not a question of singing and acting, but of *being* Don Giovanni, Rodolfo, Boris Godounow—how can anything but complete freedom of mind, deep inner relaxation, produce the miraculous transformation? How can the singer travel to the lofty heights of artistic perfection if he is weighted down by a cumbersome German grammar and a set of Victor recordings teaching him how to pronounce *l'amour?*

There ought to be a law to stop these crimes against music, drama, humanity—and special legislation should provide slow garroting for Madame Pemideli, a singing coach of my acquaintance. Madame Pemideli is a Greek married to an Italian who teaches American singers German roles. I heard one of her pupils sing Sieglinde. When I went over to tell Madame that I thought she ought to be shot, addressing her, of course, in the language of Richard Wagner, she got up and thanked me profusely in Dutch. She didn't know a single word of the language she had instilled in two hundred and fifty of her flock.

Miss Bishop's next offering is marked "Bloomington— University of Indiana." It contains very unusual things. There is first the story of Kurt Weill's *Down in the Valley,* the school opera he wrote as the American counterpart to his *Jasager.* It was performed for the first time in Bloomington in the summer of 1948. Kurt came up for the performance and brought along Marion Bell, a lovely Broadway star, who took the lead in the play—all the remainder of the cast being students of the university. Weill was visibly moved by the event: that a town in the

American "hinterland" should give the world première of one of his works was deeply significant to him who had such a keen, never-failing sense for the trends of the contemporary theater. Since then Bloomington has been host to other world premières: Lukas Foss' *Jumping Frog*, for example, or Walter Kaufmann's drugstore comedy *A Parfait for Irene*, or the first stage presentation of television's first-born opera, Menotti's miraculous *Amahl*.

This latest type of opera house in the new American style is also the scene of the "Hoosier Parsifal," produced each Palm Sunday (since 1949—how new it all is, how fresh, growing and growing everywhere at the same time!) by the Opera Workshop of the School of Music. Two hundred students participate as soloists, as knights of the Holy Grail, as Flowermaidens. In supreme disregard for illusion, the roles of Parsifal and Kundry are divided between two singers each: it lightens the singing load and gives increased opportunities to more young singers. There is a sixty-piece orchestra, made up exclusively of students. Scenery and costumes are designed and executed by the art department of the university. The public comes from all over the state, its numbers increasing from year to year. Even a Parsifal supper is served, in true Bayreuth style, during a long intermission. Already the Easter Parsifal is becoming a traditional fixture of Holy Week in Indiana.

These are the facts. What is behind them? Here and in dozens of similar institutions all over the United States are the makings of what may well be called an *indirect* subsidy, a new, constructive, imaginative, and positive solution to problems that are typical of the conditions prevailing in this country today. It is true that neither the federal government nor the town of Bloomington is "subsidizing" the opera, but the state of Indiana, through its university, is paying the salary of the director and of the conductor. The university provides a magnificent auditorium, seating 3,750 people and equipped with the latest devices of stage magic. It provides the orchestra, stagehands, chorus, tailors and painters, dancers and electricians, a complete operatic ensemble, independent of the tormenting exigencies of the box office, of union demands, or pressure from press agents and concert managers.

The Hoosier Parsifal cannot be judged by the professional standards of traditional opera houses here or abroad (although it might well replace, by fastidiousness of presentation, by intensity and enthusiasm of purpose, what it lacks in training, brilliance, and routine), but as the Bloomington experience is multiplied all over America it represents a development of far-reaching and quite revolutionary potentialities. The situation—the university taking the place of the kings, archbishops, grand dukes, or city councils of Europe—is new, typical, constructive. The knights in Indiana might not sing as well as the knights at Thirty-ninth Street and Broadway (although they look much knightlier), but for the young people who went through dozens of rehearsals and the excitement of actual performances under the guidance of professional artists this is an experience never to be forgotten. They grow up actively inoculated with the excitement that only opera, that unique combination of so many art forms, can give. As they grow older, they will not forget.

Bloomington is one of the many new centers that have entered the operatic field on a fairly advanced level. But there are many outposts still camping in the wilderness, in primitive huts, fighting the mosquitoes and crocodiles of the swamps. Somewhere here should be a letter from Ludwig Zirner, a musician from Vienna who is now a member of the music faculty of the University of Illinois in Urbana. Miss Bishop! Miss Bishop!

Here is Miss Bishop. Here, of course, is the letter. Here is what Mr. Ludwig Zirner has to say:

"In the spring of 1947," he writes, "two students approached me with the request that I help them 'do an opera.' A soprano and a baritone, they had found something that fitted their voices. They wanted to perform *The Telephone* by Menotti.

"The request, evidently grown out of their need to find an outlet for an art form fitting their individual talent and interest, started us on a search towards a solution of an educational and cultural problem of far-reaching implications.

"The Opera Workshop of the University of Illinois is now in operation. Each semester the students perform in at least one evening of operatic scenes, and each school year some of them have the opportunity of performing in a complete opera, given in co-operation with the Uni-

versity of Illinois Theatre Guild. In the opera workshop
we only accept students who we feel will be able to take
active part in these performances.

"Our repertory depends on the available voices, on the
age and character of the students, and the amount of
time they have available within the academic curriculum.
Theoretically, four hours per week are spent in the opera
workshop class, for which the students receive one half-
hour credit towards their degree. Much more time, however, is spent rehearsing, for which all participants give
freely of their time. The largest amount of time is spent
on musical training. When the students have absorbed
the musical problems and gained an understanding of the
style and character of words and music, the staging of a
scene begins. Vocal production is supervised by the students' voice instructor; diction and additional vocal
coaching is handled by a highly experienced operatic
singer, now a member of our staff.

"It seems basically unsatisfactory to me to stage operatic scenes in street clothes and on a bare concert stage.
However, it is impractical to produce complete scenery
and costumes for the many selections from the operatic
literature with which we work. We have tried to solve
the problem with a device we call 'basic screen sets' and
'basic costumes.' Simple screens of various sizes are arranged to create specific acting areas. Platforms and basic
furniture are assembled on the stage. The basic costume
consists of clothing units that are interchangeable and
merely suggest the characters, the impression largely de-

pending on the method of draping and on color combinations. Thus the changing of scenery can be accomplished within a few minutes by some non-singing
members of the workshop while I introduce the following
scene and give general information on what is to follow.
We have found that these basic 'props' are more than
adequate, that the performers learn to project their parts
with great conviction, and that the props serve as an
enormous stimulus to the imagination of both the performers and the audience.

"The complete opera performances given in the university theater, usually on four consecutive nights, are
produced in the conventional proscenium theater, with
costumes designed for the specific performance. Scenery
and lighting are provided by the Theater Department of
the university. There are two singers for almost every
character in the cast, partly to avoid the strain on young
voices and partly to give more singers a chance to perform.

"This program has been successful from the artistic,
the human, and the educational point of view. It has
stimulated great interest in opera on the campus and in
the town, and as we go on we feel that we are beginning
to satisfy a cultural need of the community. We are fully
aware of our technical limitations; but the opportunity
of expressing themselves by singing and acting has attracted many who at first stood aside. It has developed
promising young voices. The understanding of the style
and character of a work of art that can only come with

active participation in its performance, the working with others in an ensemble, proves a great musical and human experience and a stimulus towards musical and intellectual growth."

Miss Bishop's last witness is a lawyer and businessman from Raleigh, North Carolina: Mr. A. J. Fletcher, a man of inspiring and contagious enthusiasm and limitless drive who best could be described as the Ludwig II of North Carolina. Almost singlehanded he started what is known as the Grass Roots Opera Movement. Its traditions go back to the very dawn of operatic life in America: to the distant year of 1949. As Opera Chairman of the North Carolina Federation of Music Clubs, King Fletcher organized a group of singers and presented operatic excerpts, preceded by a short talk on the subject on hand, throughout the state. In only two of the cities visited had an opera ever been given before.

"What I learned from the first year," the witness volunteers, "convinced me that we needed a centralized operatic group to service our territory: no one of the smaller communities could supply sufficient musicians and singers to do it locally, but every one had enough interested listeners and many a few people who wanted and were able to sing and perform in opera."

Fletcher, at his own expense, engaged a full-time director to settle down in North Carolina and to devote all his time to the development of locally produced opera. The

first production was *Cosi Fan Tutte*—in English, of
course, under the alluring title *School for Lovers*. King
Fletcher took the cast to one of his castles—a cottage on
Bogue Sound—where they lived and learned their parts.
Guglielmo was a dentist, Ferrando an accountant, Fior-
diligi a clerk on a state agency, Dorabella, a voice teacher.
The part of the philosopher Alfonso was taken by lawyer
Fletcher himself.

The Grass Roots Company has played in more than
thirty cities and towns of North Carolina. Music Clubs,
Junior Chambers of Commerce, Elks Clubs, Parent-
Teacher Associations are the sponsors—and they usually
make money on the opera. Fletcher will take his *School
for Lovers* to any point in the state for a guarantee of $60
plus 50 per cent of the profits. For *Carmen* he needs a
guarantee of $110, plus. Except for the salary of the direc-
tor, the Grass Roots Opera is self-sustaining. It has now
found official recognition of its importance and scope:
the University of North Carolina at Chapel Hill has established an opera school. It is run by the university's
extension division in co-operation with the North Carolina Federation of Music Clubs and the Grass Roots
Opera Company. Qualified students will get much more
than a college education: they will be able to sing in
actual productions with the company. It's only a grass-
roots education, a grass-roots training—a primitive beginning. But our hat is off to lawyer Fletcher down in
Raleigh who likes to play Don Alfonso in the sticks and
who hires opera singers with a cleaner heart and purer

purpose than the Grand Duke of Darmstadt, the Arch-
bishop of Salzburg, or even his royal predecessor, Ludwig
II of Bavaria himself.

Thank you, Mr. Fletcher, and thank you, Miss Bishop.
That will be all for today.

GOOD NIGHT,
MY DOVES

They are gone. I am alone. In a little while I, too, will be on my way home.

It has been a wonderful day, a day full of life, of faces, of voices, of secret messages: sparkling lights on the dark ocean of the future.

Where will it lead to? How can it fail to succeed?

It just seems to burst out of the soil, in its own good time, at its own rhythm, in its own proper place and form. Already there is a brilliant crop of American singers spilling over to many lands. They sing the lead in a new Stravinsky opera in Venice. They swim across a lake in Florence, giving out with an aria by Von Weber. They win prizes in Lausanne and make debuts in Brussels and Vienna. Even at the Met more than half the cast are Americans.

There is opera on television, opera on

tour, opera in the concert halls, opera in schools, in clubs, grand opera, just opera and opera in the lilliput stage. It is teeming with life, bubbling over with plans, fermenting, pushing ahead, growing in the fertile rain of spring: trees, flowers, tomatoes, and a lot of weeds. It is unsuppressible.

What a wonderful, heart-warming feeling to be in the midst of it. Yes, I am blessed with the miraculous recurrence of a former life. Not without purpose have I preserved the pictures on my wall, the trophies of days gone by: posters, programs, scores, memories. Here at this desk, under the pictures of Berg, Strauss, Weill, a steady and ever-increasing flood of requests for new operas comes in from workshops, opera guilds, colleges, little theaters, operas intimes, co-op operas, high schools, summer camps, music schools, operas on the roof and operas in the cellar. Again the most prominent part in the rapidly unfolding drama is reserved for the composer and the writer. Again I am tossed in the midst of the stream.

This new movement—and a movement of driving force and relentless power it is, so basically different in its history, its economics and artistic aims from the conditions that produced the traditional operatic repertoire abroad— can never make its mark on the contemporary American scene without a contemporary American repertory, without works written for the facilities, the audiences, the singers, the time, and the surroundings of America today.

Never would the American theater be the living, creative force it is if its repertory consisted only of plays by

Shakespeare, Goethe, Sheridan, Strindberg, Molière, Shaw, and Ibsen. The present generation of American composers will not be able to refuse to the musical theater what O'Neill, Tennessee Williams, Arthur Miller, Thornton Wilder, and Clifford Odets have given to the stage.

The leading composers of America grew up and rose to prominence in the decades that saw the great advance of serious music in America—the radio age, the age of symphonic pioneering, the age when a performance by the Boston Symphony Orchestra was the supreme measure of happiness, the yardstick of success and recognition. They had no artistic and certainly no financial inducement, no training, no inclination to go through the tedious process of searching for a libretto and writing the hundreds of complicated pages of an operatic score. Now, for the first time, artistic as well as financial rewards are possible. The American scene begins to look to the young composers of today as did the European scene at the dawn of "the Periclean age of the European theater," when we set out together on a magnificent, uncharted trip.

That period of a highly decentralized theater, of daring and experiment, of a great spiritual enrichment of the musical world was a period of great productivity mainly for and because of the composer. He and nobody else was in the lead. The names of the dazzling singers are forgotten, the names of producers, painters, revivers have faded away. Only the names of the creative men are alive.

This can be a great moment for the American composer. The operatic facilities lacking in the past are suddenly here. They will become broader, brighter, and more exciting as the story unfolds. It is up to him not to make compromises, not to look down on the still limited technical and artistic possibilities, but to make use of them, to raise their standards in a creative and imaginative approach. The time is here, now, for him to take the lead. He and nobody else can mold these new forces, still young, still waiting to be guided and to be inspired, to be channeled in the right or in the wrong direction.

Anything can happen.

There are no limitations. It is up to the American composer and writer to give sense and direction to the new decentralized operatic movement in America, to make it strong, powerful, and creative and into something that will live in the history of the arts.

But that will have to wait till tomorrow. It's late. The day is gone.

Turn off the lights. Close the windows. Draw the curtains. It's time to go home.

The store, downstairs, is quiet. A few scattered men still linger behind their counters, sorting music, making notes on long mysterious slips of paper, leaning, dead-tired, on empty, deserted bins. The music boxes are silent at last. The only sound comes from the tremendous bunch of keys that the night watchman swings around and around and around in a steady, tinkling hum.

Good night, my doves. I'll see you in the morning.

There will be music again, more voices coming through the sunlight and through the rain. Go to sleep now, high up on a crevice on the fortieth floor of the Chrysler Building, where the air is pure and strong, nearer the sky and the winds that blow in from the sea.

Tomorrow you'll bring me the air of the Azores, of the Pole, of Africa. The murmur of the sea, the breath of the stars, the scents of the flowers of Italy and of strange and wonderful bushes that grow in the castles of Spain.